M000313326

SUCH DIZZY
NATURAL HAPPINESS

SUCH DIZZY
NATURAL HAPPINESS

A Long Loving Look at the Lord's Prayer

To Brooke and Kathy

PATRICK HANNON, CSC

Peace!
Pat Hannon, csc

Such Dizzy Natural Happiness
A Long Loving Look at the Lord's Prayer
by Patrick Hannon, CSC

Edited by Gregory F. Augustine Pierce
Designed and typeset by Andrea Reider
Cover Image from Adobe Stock Images. Used with permission.

Copyright © 2022 by Patrick Hannon, CSC

Scripture quotations are from the *The Message: Catholic/Ecumenical Edition,* copyright ©2015 by Eugene Peterson. Licensed with permission of NavPress, represented by Tyndale House Publishers, a Division of Tyndale House Ministries, Carol Stream, Illinois 60188. All rights reserved.

Published by ACTA Publications, Chicago, Illinois, www.actapublications.com, 800-397-2282.

All rights reserved. No part of this publication may be reproduced or transmitted in any form or by any means, electronic or mechanical, including photocopying and recording, or by any information storage and retrieval system, including the Internet, without permission from the publisher. Permission is hereby given to use short excerpts with proper citation in reviews and marketing copy, bulletins and handouts, and scholarly papers.

Library of Congress Catalog number: 2022944722

ISBN: 978-0-87946-720-3

Printed in the United States of America by Total Printing Systems

Year 30 29 28 27 26 25 24 23 22

Printing 10 9 8 7 6 5 4 3 2 First

Text printed on 30% post-consumer recycled paper

CONTENTS

INTRODUCTION

LOVE SONG FOR THE CHRISTIAN WORLD

There is no need to look for God here or there.
God is no farther away than the
door of your own heart.

Meister Eckhart, *Collected Sermons*

I f I'm honest, I admit that for a good part of my life the Our Father had been like a good relief pitcher in the game of prayer: solid, dependable, workmanlike. But it wasn't my star pitcher. Any number of other go-to prayers always seemed to shine more brightly. The *Memorare* immediately comes to mind. I love that prayer, more poetry than prose. My mother, I am told, whispered the *Memorare* at parish bingo nights when she got one ink blot away from winning a game. ("Remember, O most gracious Virgin Mary, that never was it known that anyone who fled to thy protection, implored thy help, or sought thine intercession was left unaided….") Grace always builds on nature.

Many years after those bingo evenings, sitting beside my mom in the school gym, when I was happily ensconced in the seminary at Notre Dame University, we seminarians would sing another Marian prayer *a cappella*, the *Salve Regina*, at the Thursday night's *Lucinarium*—a solemn kind of night prayer. We sang it in Latin, of course. In that chant, I would be transported to a joyfully rambunctious place in my soul. It was as though all the angels, heavenly and fallen, were mingling at a long-anticipated family reunion—laughter and singing, quaffs of ale and talk of old times before the war, lots of hugs and tears.

The Our Father, on the other hand—even on those occasions when it is sung (in English or Latin)—left me feeling as though I was simply doing my duty. How wrong I was then, and this book is an attempt to right that wrong. Turns out that The Lord's Prayer, as it is also called, has always been there for me, like the driver's license in my wallet: I know I'll probably need it every time I leave the house.

Even today, as a fifty-something priest of the Holy Cross order, I know I pray the Act of Contrition ten times more often than I pray the Our Father; but that admission might be saying more than I intend. I regularly bump up against the wall (at times I plough into it) that separates the person I want to be from the person I am. Even St. Paul in his letter to the Romans over two millennia ago, noted that "the things I say I want to do, I do not do; and the things I say I don't want to do, I do." So I guess that is just part of the human

3

condition. It's not, however, a good feeling. So the Act of Contrition helps me pivot as quickly as I can from regret to gratitude, for in the end the echo of contrition tells me sin can serve a holy purpose, if we let it, by uncannily reminding us of *who* and *whose* we are: perfectly flawed human creatures, all children of the heavenly Father, utterly dependent upon the Father's all-embracing love for everything, for life and living, for breath and air. So now I try not to be too intimidated by sin. ("Who got the last word, oh, Death? Oh, Death, who's afraid of you now?" So says St. Paul in First Corinthians.) The Act of Contrition reorients me. It turns me away from the territory of sin and death and points me back to the territory of grace where I belong and to God whose merciful love has no rival.

The first half of the Hail Mary, of course, draws us into the story of the Visitation—another happy family reunion, where whatever fear Mary may have been harboring regarding the incredible circumstances of her pregnancy is banished in Elizabeth's beatitude. It's a prayer-story that has always drawn me closer to God by reminding me that God also has a maternal instinct. Even the second half of the *Ave*

Maria, as we ask Mary our mother to pray for us now and at the hour of our death, we know that the God whom Jesus taught us to call *Abba* ("Dad" or "Papa") in the *Pater Noster*, holds us tenderly, gently, as any loving mother or father would do.

The Church has given us so many other prayers, arrows that fill our spiritual quiver, which we shoot toward heaven hoping to pierce the heart of God. Yet there is only one prayer that *Jesus* taught us. It's the only prayer that the Church says we *have to have the guts* to pray. (The invitation the priest offers before we say the Our Father at Mass goes like this: "At the Savior's *command* and formed by divine teaching, we *dare* to say....")

I think this singular prayer, the Lord's own prayer, bears further exploration. This book is my hymn to the prayer in the hope you will find something new in it for yourself. The translation I use for the prayer will be the one I always use, perhaps a little dated for some, perhaps too contemporary for others. (If you love the Our Father as I do, you can easily substitute your own translation or even one of the wonderful others found in the back of the book.)

5

SUCH DIZZY NATURAL HAPPINESS

ॐ

I do not remember learning to pray the Lord's Prayer, as I do not remember my first breath or my first words. I am, of course, grateful for these liminal moments. Remove one—breath, language, prayer—and I would cease to be. As to the Our Father, I certainly would have committed it to memory by my First Holy Communion for, preceding that sacrament I would have had to have celebrated my first confession. It was a well-known fact among the older playground crowd at Our Lady of Grace School in Castro Valley, California, that our pastor, Father James Stack consistently required penitents to say three Our Fathers. (Father Stack's seemingly pro forma approach to penance—at least to us kids back then—strikes me now as both wise and kind. "Pivot as fast as you can from your sins, you have already been forgiven," he seemed to be telling us. "The Father's mercy is stronger than any sin you could possibly commit. So pray your sorrow away before the Blessed Sacrament and then go back out and play.")

Which is what we always did on those first Fridays. I would emerge from the incensed and candlelit church duly shriven and onto an asphalt playground that rang with the soothing noises of a child's triumph over darkness and defeat: the swishes of basketballs through nylon-netted hoops, the cracks of a baseball bat making contact with a just-hoping-to-curve curveball, the tinny, playful shrieks of girls being chased by boys, the generous hum of a hundred conversations about topics that rightly occupied serious-minded children—like lunch, Sister Delfina's mole, Steinberg's ability to burp the Pledge of Allegiance, and other such matters obviously more important than sin or sorrow. So, sometime before the age of six I learned the Lord's Prayer.

I imagine this was a task given to (or claimed by) my mother. When my parents divvied up their parental tasks, my father, it seems, became responsible for raising us to be responsible citizens of planet Earth and our mother to be future eternal citizens of Heaven. She clearly was the more overtly religious of the two. You can imagine how devilishly it played out in our home once it became apparent to her older, often-up-to-no-good kids that she was a pious woman. Once we put it together—how she crossed herself whenever she passed a church or heard an ambulance's siren; prayed aloud for God's help at least a dozen times a day because raising nine kids for heavenly citizenship, evidently, wasn't all that it was cracked up to be—we looked for an opportunity to have a bit of fun with her. One of my older siblings must have noticed one day that she reverently bowed her head whenever Jesus' name was uttered. "Eeeee-excellent," I must have said when the news trickled down to me.

It was one of those lazy summer afternoons. I was around ten years old and saw the opportunity to drive my mother a little crazy. Every time I bumped into her—in the kitchen cooking, in the backyard taking the sun-dried laundry down, in the living room knitting—I said, "Jesus!" And without look-ing up, she simply bowed her head and continued what she was doing. After a while, I grew a bit weary searching for her and flinging out a "Jesus" here and a "Jesus" there. So at one point I sat beside her at the dining room table where she was doing something useful, I'm sure, and I kept on simply whispering the name of Jesus. ("Jesus." [Mom bows her head.] "Jesus." [ditto] "Jesus." [ditto]). We went on like this for a while. When I got to, oh, I don't know, maybe the fortieth or fiftieth "Jesus," she paused, took a drag from her cigarette, and looked up at me. "I'll keep doing this as long as you like," she said. "Knock yourself out." I don't remember what I was thinking as I walked away, but looking back now I know what I would have wanted to have said then: "Woman, I am not worthy!"

Apparently, Mom took literally Paul's admonition to the Philippians. To appreciate my mother's response to my lame attempt at bugging her that day (and to draw a sharper focus on the power of prayer), I will quote a bit more extensively from *The Message* Bible:

Having become human, Jesus stayed human. It was an incredibly humbling process. He didn't claim special privileges. Instead, he lived a selfless, obedient life and then died a selfless, obedient death—and the worst kind of death at that: a crucifixion. Because of that obedience, God lifted him high and honored him far beyond anyone or anything, or ever, so that all created beings in Heaven and on Earth—even those long ago dead and buried—*will bow [at the name of Jesus] in worship....*"

Of course, it would take me a few decades to begin to appreciate how in that holy, physical gesture (and unspoken prayer) my mother was quietly acknowledging the greatest gift—God's graceful love enfleshed in Jesus—she had ever received. It was the gift that enabled her to get up every morning, with a gritty faith that can move mountains, and face the life that had been offered to her and the one she had accepted. It gave her the patience to love all her kids and her husband, and I suppose all the friends and strangers she encountered.

The Our Father takes this divine and enfleshed love as a given. (We cry out, "Forgive us our debts!"

and we hear back, "Okay! I already have!"). We listen more intently to that petition at the heart of the Our Father and hear echoes of the stories of forgiveness that upon their telling (and retelling) leave us more hopeful, more grateful, more humble. It is a divine gift offered to us all, every moment of every day: a sacrificial love, so pure, so complete, so generous, so seemingly *wasteful* (who among us has not tried, on more than a few occasions, to test the limits of God's love only to discover that the wellspring of God's mercy is unstoppable?) Apparently, Father Jim Schultz, a member of the novitiate staff my year as a novice, was right when he said about the merciful blood of Christ, "Not a drop is wasted." Divine mercy's unmatched ability to heal the deepest wound, bridge the greatest divide, sate the deepest hunger and thirst, makes me want to be a better person.

One day, a disciple of the Lord asked him to teach him and the others how to pray. Seems like a pretty obvious request, given that Jesus was the Son of God. What is not obvious is why he only taught his disciples this one prayer. Maybe it is because it contains everything we need.

I imagine every parent today—along with the world's lost and lonely, battered and broken—easily seeing themselves among that crowd of disciples. Give me a prayer, Jesus, upon which we can rest our weary heads, our broken hearts. Give us a prayer that we can lean into and find our balance. A prayer for the desperate, for those wondering if they're going to make it to the next day, for those who are holding on to a grudge, a wound, a failure that is slowly eating their hearts away from the inside. And Jesus did, genius that he was. "With a God like Our Father loving us," Jesus pointed out, "we can pray very simply. Like this…."

The Our Father is uttered billions of times every day in churches and chapels, for sure, but also in every conceivable place and time. Think of the one place the Our Father could never possibly be uttered or heard, and I am sure it's been prayed there: bars, brothels, execution chambers, battlefields, ballparks, outer space, maybe your kitchen table or bedroom. It embodies the Spirit, Paul tells us in the Letter to the Romans, that moves us in moments of fear to cry out, "Abba, Father!" It recalls these verses from Psalm 139:

"Is there any place I can go to avoid your Spirit? to be out of your sight? If I climb to the sky, you're there! If I go underground, you're there! If I flew on morning's wings to the far western horizon, You'd find me in a minute—you're already there waiting! Then I said to myself, 'Oh, God even sees me in the dark! At night I'm immersed in the light!' It's a fact: darkness isn't dark to you; night and day, darkness and light, they're all the same to you."

Most days I pray the Our Father three times as a Holy Cross priest (at Mass and at morning prayer and evening prayer). My usual penance from my confessor is to find a quiet place and sing the Our Father, making up my own melody. So there's a minimum of twelve more recitations a year. And I'm not counting the times when I have prayed it before the captain of the jet in whose fuselage I'm trapped revs the engines just before taking off. (I also pray the Hail Mary and the Act of Contrition at take offs. I like to think such last-minute prayers reflect a calm and sturdy faith, but I can't help seeing in them more than a hint of dread and an attempt to buy some more time on Earth.) Slowly I've come to appreciate the power of this one prayer, how it draws me out of myself and toward some deep eternal truth—moth to holy flame, you might say—that I might lose myself in the penetrating light of God.

Jesus taught his disciples—including you and me—only this stripped-down-to-the-chassis prayer. In English, Saint Luke's version in his Gospel is a mere fifty-five words. The Semitic-language version is even shorter. It's a prayer meant for sojourners who must travel light. And yet, unpacking that prayer, spending time in the Zen garden of those fifty-five words, might draw each of us ever closer—not only the power of the Lord's Prayer, but to prayer itself.

The scholar George Palmer called the Our Father the "love song for the Christian world." Writer James Thirtle spoke of it as the "pearl of prayers and the fountain-prayer, from whence flows all other Christian prayers." Between the lines of this prayer, imbedded into its words, twined to every syllable, are rich stories of faith stronger than fear; of mercy greater than the fiercest grudge; of a Father, *our* Father, who lives eternally at the door of our hearts. We need only to open it up.

Patrick Hannon, CSC
University of Portland
Portland, Oregon
165th Anniversary of the
Holy Cross Brothers and Priests

I

STRONG IN THE BROKEN PLACES

"The human animal is a beast that must die.
If he's got money,
he buys and buys and buys everything he can,
in the crazy hope one of those things
will be life-everlasting,
which it can never be."

Big Daddy Pollitt, from *Cat on a Hot Tin Roof*
by Tennessee Williams

Nicholas Green, a seven-year-old, reddish-brown-haired, freckled boy from Bodega Bay, California, was sleeping in the back seat of a rental car with his four-year-old sister, Eleanor, while their mom, Maggie, and dad, Reg, sat up front, happily driving a stretch of Italian highway that connects Salerno to Reggio Calabria. It was late one Thursday night in October 1994. They were making their way back to their rented vacation villa in Sicily, but bandits—apparently thinking the Greens were jewelers—began following them. At one point they approached the Green's car and began shouting at them in Italian, a language neither parent was fluent in. Instinctively, Reg sped up in his attempt to evade them. The bandits shot at the car from behind several times and then abandoned their pursuit. It was only when Reg pulled the car over a few miles later that he and Maggie realized that Nicholas had been shot in the head. He was pronounced dead a few days later in a Messina hospital. When Maggie and Reg realized that Nicholas could not be saved, it was Maggie who said, "Shouldn't we donate Nicky's organs?"

Francesco Mondello and Domenica Galleta received Nicholas' corneas, and with them their eyesight. Tino Motta and Anna Maria Di Ceglie received his kidneys. Maria Pia Pedala, nineteen years old, received his liver. Maria then married her childhood sweetheart and a year later they had a baby boy whom they named Nicholas. Silvia Ciampi got his pancreas. And Andrea Mongiardo, fifteen years old, weighing a frail sixty pounds and on life support, received Nicholas' heart. When the Italian media first asked Maggie how she felt about her son's heart being transplanted into another boy's chest, she said: "I always hoped Nicholas would have a long life. Now I hope his heart has a long life." Later, Andrea would tell his sister that his new heart was "a Ferrari."

"There's a sadness that was never there before. I'm never completely happy anymore," Reg Green said in an interview a few years ago. "Even when I'm at my happiest, I think: 'Wouldn't it be better if Nicholas was here?'" Still, the *l'effetto Nicholas*—the Nicholas Effect—has brought Reg and Maggie and Eleanor some peace. And before Nicholas' tragic death and the Greens' decision to donate Nicholas' organs, Italy trailed every European country in organ donation. Now they are in the top third.

And in Bodega Bay, California, just off Highway One, perhaps a ten-minute walk from the Pacific Ocean, you'll see a bell tower called "The Children's Belltower." In Nicholas' honor, his hometown erected this memorial. It consists of three nested towers, with 140 mismatched bells hanging from steel crossbars. The majority were donated from Italian schools, churches, ships, and mines, all to show their affection and gratitude for the Green's selfless, merciful decision. The center bell, made by the prestigious Marinelli foundry that has been forging papal bells for over a thousand years, bears an inscription of the names of the organ recipients. Pope John Paul II blessed the bells himself, and the Italian president and prime minister paid their own respects, arranging for all the bells to be flown to California by the Italian Air Force. Today, a soft ocean breeze is enough to get the bells to chime.

I try to imagine what those bells sound like when that salty Pacific breeze touches them. I hear playful, innocent voices. I hear gentle laughter borne of joy—the tenor of which suggests a hard-fought victory of some kind, a kind of release, an unfurling. The chorus of those bells hint of the merciful voice of our Father, who knows what it feels like to lose a child, whose love is strong enough to triumph over any defeat, any darkness of any kind. And so it begins.

"Our Father."

When I think of God as Father (in Aramaic it is rendered *Abba,* perhaps best understood in English as "Dad" or "Papa"), I immediately think of the father character in Jesus' parable of the prodigal son. In fact, you might say the father is the prodigal one—throwing his stupid, sinful son a party with the proverbial fatted calf.

This younger of two sons, we remember, has demanded his inheritance from his father. (Jesus' listeners would have dropped their jaws hearing this. What a scandalous beginning! What a fantastic lead!) The son was essentially telling his father, "I don't care if you are alive or dead, give me my money." Given the Jewish cultural norms of the time, the father-son relationship in that instant would have been irreparably torn. And indeed it was. For the son, there was no going back.

Time passes, however, and the son, now broken and destitute, having thrown away his fortune on booze and sex workers, does attempt to return home. His hope is that his father will treat him as a slave and therefore at least he will not starve to death, with his naked corpse found some day on some blighted street in a strange town. The kid knew, as he made the last turn onto the road that led to his father's home, that there was no going back to the way things were.

It strikes many that in a way the younger son was still taking his father for a sucker. As far as we can tell from the story, he had not changed or matured in any significant way. Since mercy was impossible (notice the son never *asks* his father for forgiveness), he was going to take advantage of what he still perceived to be his father's soft and gullible heart.

By this reading, too, we might begin to appreciate the older son's less-than-gracious reaction to the grand party his father was putting on to celebrate his brother's return. ("You've *got* to be kidding me, Dad.

Can't you see? This *jerk of a son* is playing you again! And you're throwing him a party? Give me a break.") This parable, though, is not about God's justice, at least the kind of justice Jesus' listeners then (and perhaps now) understood.

But there the father was, evidently, where he had been every day since his younger son departed: looking out from the front porch for any sign of his wayward boy. Here's how Luke tells it in *The Message* Bible:

> When he was still a long way off, his father saw him. His heart pounding, he ran out, embraced him, and kissed him. The son started his speech: "Father, I've sinned against God, I've sinned before you; I don't deserve to be called your son ever again." But the father wasn't listening. He was calling to the servants, "Quick. Bring a clean set of clothes and dress him. Put the family ring on his finger and sandals on his feet. Then get a grain-fed heifer and roast it. We're going to feast! We're going to have a wonderful time! My son is here—given

up for dead and now alive! Given up for lost and now found!" And they began to have a wonderful time.

The prodigal father restores his lost son to full filial relationship. It is as though the boy had never left. This parable ushers in a paradigm shift of such magnitude that we must, upon hearing the story, recalibrate our understanding of who God is in the moral universe, a new view of the God-as-Father that aligns with Jesus' radical understanding: *His* Father's justice is *always* mercy.

Jesus, however, leaves us with the image of the prodigal father begging his older son to come join the party, to see in his brother's return to full sonship a pathway to his own salvation. but the parable ends before we know if the elder son ever sheds the hard carapace of resentment and anger and fear that protects him from what Dietrich Bonhoeffer called the "costly grace" of unconditional love.

My friend, Fr. Bill Burke, says that the reason Jesus leaves the parable dangling like this is that *we* are *all* the second son, and *we* have to decide whether we want a father/God who is "fair" or one who is "generous to the point prodigality." I hope the older kid did go into the party. I hope I always do. I hope you always do. In the end, the only thing, as far as I can tell, that can reconcile enemies—and make no mistake, the older brother saw his younger brother ("that son of YOURS!") as an enemy—is the moment when we can, with a new set of eyes, see in the other our cherished sibling and thus acknowledge that we all share the same spiritual DNA that unites us to our Creator, whom Jesus told us is everyone's—Christian and non-Christian alike—*shared* Abba.

As Pope Francis put it recently: "If I am not at peace with my brothers and sisters, I cannot say 'Father' to God. We cannot pray with enemies in our hearts."

૮૪૦

In my early priesthood, I wrestled with much of the patriarchal language of the Church, how in its interpretation of scripture and in its liturgical life faithful women were often excluded, especially from accessing the full power of the revealed Word, which if you read the Bible carefully seems to go *out of its way* to *include* women.

I recognized and appreciated the number of feminine images of God found in the Bible (From Isaiah 49, for instance: "Can a mother forget the infant at her breast, walk away from the baby she bore? But even if mothers forget, I'd never forget you—never.") And I saw clearly how Jesus seemed intent on breaking down the barriers that kept women from experiencing their full personhood.

I have over the years, then, tried to be sensitive to pronouns and images when I refer to God in my preaching and teaching. But I have to say I've also been queasy about messing with the language of the Our Father. Virtually all scripture scholars agree that the word Jesus used in the prayer he taught was *Abba*.

In the light of the parable of The Prodigal Son, then, perhaps we can agree on a couple of things. First, the image Jesus creates of the prodigal father is an affectionate and doting one. The character lacks any hint of what we would call today toxic masculinity. Jesus' understanding of his Father in Heaven stands in *stark* contrast to any number of the harsh, warring, and violent images of God found in the scriptures.

Perhaps we can also agree that our understanding of God as 'Father' is a metaphorical one. Theologically, God does not have a gender. (Dare we say, God *transcends* gender.) So as far as the Our Father goes, I'm content to hold onto the word Jesus used and to find in it a new way of understanding God, particularly in the context of the prayer Jesus taught us. Jesus' understanding of his *Abba* and the *Abba* he revealed to his disciples and through them to us, is radically tender, loving, open. My own father, a good and loving man, abided, it seems to me, by the dominant masculine norms of his time. He was outwardly and often affectionate toward my mother but rarely toward his children, particularly his sons. I do not love him less for it. But who was it that first showed me that fathers could be affectionate? Jesus.

In his final discourse with his disciples in John's Gospel, before he walked the road to Calvary, Jesus actually was praying aloud to the Father as a Son who knew in his bones that his Father loved him beyond measure, that God's promise of a life beyond death could be trusted in the face of great suffering. It's a deeply intimate moment we become privy to. These were the last words Jesus spoke that Passover meal: "Righteous Father, the world has never known you, But I have known you, and these disciples know that you sent me on this mission. I have made your very being known to them—who you are and what you do—and continue to make it known, so that your love for me might be in them exactly as I am in them."

This was the communion the father in the parable was inviting his older son into—a relationship not built on justice and fairness as the world sees it but on forgiveness and tender mercy that confounds the proud and gives succor to the weary. In his reflection on The Prodigal Son in his *Confessions*, Augustine at one point is referring to all of us, we children of our one Father, but he might as well have been speaking about the two brothers: "Let them turn and see that you are there…and throw themselves upon your mercy and rest upon your breast after the difficult ways which they have trod. And you in your gentleness wipe the tears from their eyes."

This image slays me. I stand in the shadow of the brothers' healing hug and wonder how mercy is even possible. Against all the dark forces mobilized to divide "them" and "us"—hatred and indifference and fear and self-centeredness and ignorance— there stands *Abba*, our mercy-filled *Abba*, steadfast on the porch still, looking out upon the seemingly endless throng of lost souls—we among them—inching toward him, stripped of virtue and any vestige of hope save a sliver, ready to welcome us all home, ready to give us our heart's deepest desire. This is the Father whom Jesus asks us to pray to and whose party he invites us into.

My mother told my father it was time. She should know. She had eight children already, in nine years. It was the evening of November 10, 1963, the day before my fourth birthday, a Sunday. My sister Sally, nine years old at the time, told me later we were watching *Bonanza* (a popular 1960s TV Western series) on the television in my parents' room. Coincidentally, I later discovered, that episode begins with the patriarch, Ben, finding Hoss (one of his three sons) in the barn waiting for a mare to give birth. I must have been riveted by the drama playing out on that old black and white Magnavox, less so by the one taking place under my nose.

Our father came in and told us he was taking Mom to the hospital. She was going to have the baby. I remember nothing of that night or early morning. I must have gone to bed sometime after the television show. Our babysitter Anna—a middle-aged, no-nonsense, drill sergeant of a woman who took care of us occasionally—must have been called into service to mind us, to keep us from tearing the house apart, which we were often wont to do in our parents' absence. She would have marched me to my bed.

I see my parents now in the station wagon (a white one we kids had nicknamed "Lightning") making their way down our street, cutting through the evening fog that obscured the window-lit homes of our neighborhood, making them all appear a bit sinister and foreboding. I can see my mom's hands pressed lightly upon her belly. She says, "Step on it,

Bill," and Dad's right foot presses down on the gas pedal and they speed past Romley's Market and Carl's Drugstore and the town's park and then pull into the emergency room parking lot of Eden Hospital, where four years before, my mom entered and soon gave birth to me: a month premature, with pneumonia clogging my tiny lungs, which almost killed me, where Fr. Stack came and baptized me as I lay in an incubator.

I see my father pacing the waiting room in the early hours of November 11. He's thirty-five years old, still lean, with tight farmer muscles, though he left the farm years ago and had become a lawyer. Occasionally he sits and reads from whatever book or section of the Sunday *Tribune* he may have brought with him. He's marking the time, wondering why the birth seems to be taking longer than usual. I see the double doors that connect the emergency room to the waiting room swing open. I see a doctor in green scrubs—his face mask resting below his neck—approach my father. He tells my father they had encountered a nuchal cord around the baby's neck—not an uncommon occurrence, by the way, one that is usually easily remedied—and it had cut off oxygen to the baby's brain. They couldn't save him. I'd like to think the doctor had placed his hand on my father's shoulder to comfort him, but it's 1963, and I am of the opinion—probably wrong—that most doctors then had a cool, detached temperament.

"Can I see my wife?" I hear my father say. "Sure," the doctor says, "once we get her into recovery." I see my father now, holding onto something, anything, to keep his balance. I do not see him cry. But I can see through him to the osseous cage inside of which his heart is swinging back and forth, beating to the rhythm of a New Orleans' funeral drum, slow, mournful. I see my dad's heart breaking.

How did my mother and father recover from that loss? Dad came home later that morning when the older kids were awake and getting ready for school. My oldest brother told me years later that when one of the older ones asked if the baby was a boy or a girl, my father said, simply, "The baby died." Apparently, these were the only words my father ever said about that day. When I was a teenager, I brought the subject up with my mother one morning while she was deep-frying chicken legs and breasts for a picnic later in the day. "I knew it was time," she told me, "but the doctor kept on telling me that we had time. They waited too long." *Those bastards*, I remember thinking. *They killed my little brother.*

After getting us breakfast and dropping the older kids off at school, my father went to his office. He put in a full day—ten appointments, plus a visit to the hospital. I know this because years later, my mother gave each of us kids—after his death—our father's day-planner from the year of our birth. I also got the one from 1963, the year my little brother James Joseph came into the world—on my birthday—stillborn. I am sure my father came home at 5:00 PM on the dot that day. We could set our watches to his homecoming each weeknight. He dropped his briefcase onto the stereo console by the front door, made it to his green-leathered chair, sat in it, placed his legs on the matching ottoman and crossed them, told one of us to turn on the news, and read the evening *Daily Review*. It strikes me now that my father must have found his balance—lest he career off the road and land in a ditch of crippling grief—by doing what he always did: With a steady, consistent and comforting hand, he guided us, his brood, into a world that, as Hemingway once wrote in *A Farewell to Arms*, "will break everyone, and afterward many are strong in the broken places."

My father's and mother's relative silence on the matter of the stillborn death of my brother seems to be now a merciful act. A child's death, perhaps more than any other tragedy, exposes the deep fault lines of a world, a universe—and by extension, God—that seem, at best, indifferent to human suffering. It is, of course, a heart-numbing conundrum as old as the story of Job. We must, it seems to me, reject easy, dismissive answers, or those that essentially let God—who, Jesus tells us, is all-merciful—off the hook. Loving God practically means letting God be God. That my father and mother got up the next morning and tried to fulfill the work entrusted to them by God—to be loving spouses to each other and good parents to their kids—even as they quietly grieved, tells me that for them trusting that *Abba's* love is stronger than even death was a choice they made, as best they could, every day.

QUESTIONS FOR REFLECTION AND DISCUSSION

1. Remember a time in your own life when you experienced great loss or sorrow. How did you handle it? What was your prayer like then?

2. What does "unconditional" love mean to you? Name three people whom you have observed loving unconditionally. Give examples of how they did it.

3. What are your problems with imagining God as a "prodigal father"? What is another image that might work better for you? Does the Lord's Prayer offer you a way of "lifting up your mind and heart" to a power greater than yourself? Why or why not?

II

I ARISE TODAY

And for all this, nature is never spent;
There lives the dearest freshness
deep down things;
And though the last lights off the black West went
Oh, morning, at the brown brink eastward,
springs—Because the Holy Ghost over the bent
World broods with warm breast and
with ah! bright wings.

Gerard Manley Hopkins, *God's Grandeur*

I was in Sydney, Australia, a number of years ago giving some lectures. One afternoon, I had lunch with a Benedictine nun, and she told me this true story. A childless couple from Sydney adopted an infant boy from a Sydney orphanage. The boy was from one of the tribes of the Indigenous Peoples. The boy grew, attended local schools, rode a bike, made friends in the neighborhood. One day—when the boy was around five or six—he and his father were walking in downtown Sydney. They encountered an old native artist selling his paintings on the sidewalk. The boy was fascinated as he inspected the paintings, mostly of landscapes richly detailed in deep shades of orange and red and brown. The boy asked the old man if he could teach him how to paint like that. The old man leaned forward. Their noses almost touched. "You already know how to," the old man said. The next day, the boy's father bought him all the art supplies he would need: paints and paintbrushes, an easel, canvas and paper.

The boy got painting. His parents marveled at the boy's—and eventually the young man's—artistic eye. He painted landscape after landscape: hills and mountains and skies of some outback region of Australia. The ones he liked especially, he framed and hung in his home. The rest, most of them, he threw out. The young man died tragically in a car accident when he was nineteen. Apparently, it is the custom among the Indigenous Peoples that they be buried in the ground where they were born. The parents were able to locate the small town where the boy had been born, a two-day's drive from Sydney.

On the morning of the second day of driving, as they got closer to the remote town, the father suddenly noticed something. He asked his wife to stop. They both got out of the car and gazed upon the rolling hills, the clear, cobalt-blue skies, the stark and tangled brush before them. "Do you see what I see?" the man said. "Oh, my God," the woman said. They had seen this landscape before. It was framed and hanging over their fireplace mantle at home. Their beautiful boy—having never been back to his ancestral home since his birth—had painted the landscape his adopted parents were now gazing upon. His Indigenous relatives were not surprised. He had painted it from memory, they would say.

The Indigenous Peoples of Australia have an ancient, eternal memory. They call it "Dreamtime." It is a memory that connects them to all those who have gone before them and to Mother Earth from which they were birthed. It's an eternal memory of an eternal story that dwells just below the surface of things, they say. We Christians have a name for this phenomenon too: We call it God, and so we continue.

"Our Father, who art in Heaven."

I was in my first year of theological studies at the University of Notre Dame when my father passed away. It was a Wednesday. I would fly back home for the funeral the following day. Late that Wednesday afternoon, Father Bob Antonelli, my spiritual director (and a Holy Cross priest) and I went on a car ride on the back roads of northern Indiana. It was autumn and the corn fields we passed—at sunset they gleamed in a woolen blanket of golden yellow—were ripe and ready for harvest. I shared stories about my dad, and Bob listened intently as he negotiated the sometimes-bumpy road. At one point, I asked him what he thought Heaven was like. "I think," and he paused for a moment, "I think it will be like one eternal hug." I looked over at him. He was smiling, looking straight ahead, into the mid-distance, as though he were, at that moment, gazing upon what he had just imagined.

I prefer the more informal, almost familial term "hug" that Bob employed in that moment, instead of the more abstract "embrace" or, even worse, "beatific vision." Perhaps it's because it aligns more with my own experience of reunions and other gatherings where friends and family assemble after a period of absence.

Just the other day, for example, my brother Brian and I were at a Peet's Coffee and Tea waiting for our beverages. A fellow in his mid-twenties appeared out of nowhere. "Joe, is that you?" A guy—also in his mid-twenties—standing in front of us turned around, and his eyes lit up and a smile took over his face. This other fellow (he had what I refer to these days as a Covid beard: rather long and scraggly and ready to be shaved when we get the all clear) came up and bear-hugged him. I delighted in being a quiet witness to their hug (see, "embrace" just doesn't do it). "How long has it been?" the guy with the beard said." "Hell," the other said, "three years?" Their chat began and was soon absorbed by the ambient hum of the shop. I smiled and my mind turned to thoughts of Heaven.

Of course, I realized a long time ago that Bob "ruined" me to hugs. Whenever I see one or hug and am hugged by someone, I think of Heaven. I may have already been drawn to such a powerful tactile image years ago: When I was a sophomore in college, my friends and I came up with a fun, late-night weekend activity. We would pile into a car and head out to the Portland airport, where we would make our way passed security (ah, the good old days) and then to a gate where a jet had just taxied up. One of us—we took turns—would slyly insert himself or herself into the stream of passengers emerging from the gate entrance. Then, when we saw our classmate, the rest of us would scream and jump up and down in delight, as though we hadn't been together in years. I think one time we actually made "Welcome Home!" signs. We would rush toward our friend and all hug, creating a scene we hoped would bring a little joy into what we assumed was a weary peripatetic populace. For what is it—beside sleeping finally in our own beds—we most look forward to after a long journey, if not a good hug?

Saint Augustine of Hippo, in his treatise on the Trinity, referred to the Father, Son, and Holy Spirit, as "Lover, Beloved, and the Love that binds them." Another way we can say this is that our Father, who is in Heaven, and the Son, who came to Earth, are eternally hugging each other in the Spirit. Both are forever giving (sacrificing) completely of themselves and eternally receiving the other in love. This wellspring of eternal and mutual self-sacrifice and eternal receiving is what makes human love possible. How else can two humans wed, that is, intertwine their lives, minds, bodies, hearts, souls—an act so selfless it doesn't seem humanly impossible—without somehow *knowing* that they have become a sacrament, a visible sign of God's presence in the world? The horizon of their pledged love extends now beyond the edges of their noses and touches a heavenly, eternal love.

Images of eternal life, of Heaven, abound. I do enjoy unfettering my imagination upon the subject occasionally: I see miles of full bookshelves, baseball diamonds, barrels of Burgundy wine. But I suspect, as St. Paul did in his first letter to the Corinthians ("No one's ever seen or heard anything like this, never so much as imagined anything quite like it—what God has arranged for those who love him"); any heavenly image I can conjure comes up—woefully and thankfully—short with what I hope will be the reality. I do have a hunch, though, that it will *feel* something like a hug-fest.

Her mother must have known that I would be videotaping her little girl that morning. She had clearly dressed her child for the occasion. As I recall, the first-grade girl from Saint Joseph Catholic School in South Bend, Indiana, let's call her Madeline, was sitting quietly in a chair when I entered the room. I was there to interview a dozen or so first graders for a project I was working on—about faith development in early childhood—in my final year of theological studies at the University of Notre Dame. I would be asking the kids various questions about God, Jesus, faith, church, etc. Madeline was the first one up to bat. She wore a starched white cotton dress with a belt. Her black patent leather shoes had been polished and a couple ribbons rested on the top of her head. Her hands rested on her lap. Her feet did not reach the floor. I introduced myself and asked her what her name was. She smiled at me shyly. Adorable.

We got right to it. I pressed the record button on the video camera that rested on a tripod set up behind me and sat down and proceeded to ask the questions I had prepared, taking notes as well. At one point my questioning turned to the subject of God the Father. (She knew the Our Father by heart.) "Can you see the Father?" I asked. "Yes," Madeline said, still smiling. "Is the Father here right now?" I asked. I was going off script. Madeline's brows furrowed slightly, as though my question seemed to her ridiculous. "Of course," she said. "Where is God the Father right now?" I pressed.

Madeline looked at a space above her head. "He's right there," she said in a whisper. Then she bent forward and looked at a space beneath her chair. "He's there," she said. She looked behind her and said God was there. She faced me again and said God was right in front of her. She then indicated to me that God was on her left and on her right. And then, finally, almost dramatically, she pointed to the part of her chest where behind skin, muscle, and bone her beating heart reclined, she said, "And God's here too!"

It struck me later, as I was reviewing the tape, that Madeline had, essentially, paraphrased part of the prayer we call the Saint Patrick Breastplate, a hymn attributed to Saint Patrick written in the style of a druidic incantation for protection on a journey. It begins, "I arise today / Through a mighty strength, the invocation of the Trinity, / Through belief in the Threeness, / Through confession of the Oneness / of the Creator of creation."

And the prayer ends this way:

I ARISE TODAY

Christ with me,
Christ before me,
Christ behind me,
Christ in me,
Christ beneath me,
    Christ above me,
Christ on my right,
Christ on my left,
Christ when I lie down,
Christ when I sit down,
Christ when I arise,
Christ in the heart of everyone
    who thinks of me,
Christ in the mouth of everyone
    who speaks of me,
Christ in every eye that sees me,
Christ in every ear that hears me.
I arise today
Through a mighty strength,
    the invocation of the Trinity,
Through belief in the Threeness,
Through confession of the Oneness
    of the Creator of creation.

Astronomers and astrophysicists remind us that what we see of the visible universe with either our naked eye or with the aid of a regular telescope is only a tiny sliver of what is out there. With advanced instruments, though, such as the Hubble telescope and the even newer Webb Space telescope, we can capture infrared, microwave, and radio waves as well. The universe becomes astonishingly kaleido-scopic. We can hardly take in the unfathomable distances of time and space, the drama of ancient galaxies colliding, of stars exploding, of black holes slurping up gravity.

And there I was one weekday morning, sitting in a classroom interviewing a little girl in a starched white dress who told me that she could see the Father whom, sadly, I could not. What set of eyes did she have that I did not?

I believed she *could* see God the Father, by the way. I absolutely believed her. Irish poet Patrick Kavanagh said, in his masterful poem *The Great Hunger*: "Men build their heavens as they build their circles /

Of friends. God is in the bits and pieces of Everyday /
A kiss here and a laugh again, and sometimes tears, /
A pearl necklace round the neck of poverty."

Madeline reminded me the border that separates
Heaven and Earth is porous for some people whose
lives are tethered to gardens where they can dig with
their hands, to forests or bodies of water, to the steady
rhythm of tides and seasons. (Poet and naturalist
Wendell Berry would refer to such folk as *placed people*: "those forever attached to the look of the sky, the
smell of native plants, and the vernacular of home.")

In the case of Madeline and her fellow tribe-children, their lives are marked by a gutsy openness to
all things spiritual; they are, for a time, endowed
with a sparkling wonder of a world that is beyond
their ability to put into words. For them, the border that marks their spiritual and material worlds is
unguarded, wide open, and "hallowed."

"Let heaven and nature sing," goes the Christmas hymn's refrain. You burrow your head into the
recess of your friend's shoulder and take in—as a
revelation—the musky or perfumed scent; you feel
the muscles of your wife's, mother's, sister's arms

tighten around your waist; you feel your father's hand press your head, tenderly, closer to him. And, for a moment, if you're open to experiencing it, you receive a hint of what Heaven will be like.

It is in this territory of grace where Heaven and Earth kiss, as they do in Psalm 85 from *The Message* Bible: "See how close his salvation is to those who fear him! Our country is home base for Glory! / Love and Truth meet in the street, Right Living and Whole Living embrace and kiss! / Truth sprouts green from the ground, Right Living pours down from the skies! / Oh yes! God gives Goodness and Beauty; our land responds with Bounty and Blessing. / Right Living strides out before him, and clears a path for his passage."

God the Father indeed reigns in highest Heaven, adored for all eternity by all the hosts and dominions of angels and archangels. At Mass, when we are united with one another at the altar of Eucharist, we join the Father, Son, and Holy Spirit and all the patriarchs and matriarchs and saints who have gone before us in the heavenly banquet feast of God's victory over sin and death. In praying the *Sanctus*, we actually join the seraphim and cherubim as they and we sing together, "Holy, Holy, Holy!" The altar of any chapel or church, though it can be measured in feet and inches, is big enough to gather all of Heaven and Earth.

We often speak, metaphorically or literally of Heaven as an unreachable place, far beyond our mortal touch. Madeline, and that young Indigenous Australian boy, indeed, any child given the chance, will tell us that—if we want to—if we have the daring, adventurous will of a child—we *can* see God, we *can* travel to that territory of grace where Heaven and Earth touch, and we *can* paint the landscape of where we came from and where we are going.

QUESTIONS FOR DISCUSSION AND REFLECTION

1. List three images or metaphors you have of Heaven. Why did you pick each of them?

2. The word *mystical* comes from the same root as *mystery*, which connotes something "secret" or

"hidden" or "unknown" or "unknowable." Describe a mystical experience you have had, once or many times.

3. How do you feel or react when you or someone else prays to a "Father" who is in "Heaven"?

III

FRESH EARTH GLEAMING

"I think it pisses God off if you walk by the color purple in a field somewhere and don't notice it. People think pleasing God is all God cares about. But any fool living in the world can see it always trying to please us back."

Shug Avery, from *The Color Purple*
by Alice Walker

Moses, as the biblical story goes, was minding his father-in-law's flock near Mount Horeb ("The Mountain of God," also known as Mount Sinai) when he encountered a burning bush that was "blazing away, but it didn't burn up." Moses heard someone shouting "Moses! Moses!" from the bush, and, indeed, as Moses approached, God ordered him: "Don't come any closer. Remove your sandals from your feet. You're standing on holy ground." God then announced, "I am the God of your father…the God of Abraham, the God of Isaac, the God of Jacob." At once, recognizing that he was in the presence of the divine, Moses hid his face; for as everyone back then knew, if you saw God's face you would surely die.

You might recall later in the Book of Exodus, when Moses was on the top of Mount Sinai and asked to "see God's glory," God said: "No one can see me and live." God then said, "Look, here is a place right beside me. Put yourself on this rock. When my glory passes by, I'll put you in the cleft of the rock and cover you with my hand until I've passed by. Then I'll take my hand away and you'll see my back. But you won't see my face."

God told Moses from the burning bush that he had been chosen to be the one to tell the Egyptian pharaoh to free all the Hebrew slaves. Moses balked at such a mission. (Who wouldn't, especially if, like Moses, you had a bad speech impediment?) But once God assured Moses that he need not worry, Moses asked the only question left to ask: "If I go to the Israelites and say to them, 'The God of your ancestors has sent me to you,' and they ask me, 'What is his name?' What do I tell them?" God replied to Moses: "I am who I am." Then God added: "This is what you will tell the Israelites: 'I AM has sent me to you.'"

"Our Father, who art in Heaven, hallowed be thy name."

I AM. God's holy name. As a writer and writing teacher who falls in love regularly with words and sentences, I have been captivated by the self-assigned name God revealed to Moses a few millennia ago. The essence of divinity itself—which by definition has to be marked by complete freedom and unfettered action—can be distilled down to two words (I am) comprised of three letters, at least in English. In Hebrew it is four letters, which are translated into six English letters as "Yahweh." Out of deep respect and awe for the name of God, the Jewish people never utter God's name, seen in the Hebrew scriptures as the tetragrammaton "YHWH"—and instead employ the title *Adonai* (LORD) when referring to God. Though it is still debated, many biblical scholars understand "YHWH" etymologically as a Hebrew form of the verb "to be," suggesting "causes to be, creates."

The whole point of this riddle is that it resists any attempt at definition! Given our human tendency to define and delineate everything and everyone as a way of controlling them, this is certainly a genius name to give yourself, if you are God ("Don't box me in / I told you not to / Don't box me in" goes the refrain from the 1983 Ridgeway/Copeland hit.) For then the unfathomable mystery (and glory) of God remains, as it must, a healthy distance beyond our puny thinking and imagination. The incomparable spiritual writer Annie Dillard put it this way, correctly

I think: "One turns at last even from glory itself with a sigh of relief. From the depths of mystery, and even from the heights of splendor, we bounce back and hurry for the latitudes of home."

Think for a moment of a few of those precious instances when God's glory breaks through and changes the trajectory of a life, when one is reduced to tears—joyful, sometimes heart-wrenching—the human body's reaction to ineffable glory: a baby's birth; her first coo; his first steps; the day your child leaves home for good; that heart-stopping first glance from across the room; falling in love for the first time; that first kiss; the moment when forgiveness weaves a passable bridge that spans, graciously, what one first thought was a permanent divide; that sunrise over Bryce Canyon, that sunset at the Cliffs of Moher, that forest walk in foggy Mount Sutro, a solitude bathed in the aroma of eucalyptus and loamy earth ("The world is charged with the grandeur of God," wrote Gerard Manley Hopkins). These and so many divinely "charged" moments act as a kind of spiritual defibrillator ("Ready? Clear!") that gets our weary or broken hearts thumping joyously again.

"Hallowed be thy name!" the Our Father says. Another way of putting it is this: "Glorify *your* name, O LORD!" And how does God glorify God's name? Through and in *us* and in *all* of God's creation. I'm thinking now of what Saint Irenaeus once wrote: "Life *in* a human being is the glory of God; the life *of* a human being is the vision of God."

At the heart of every healthy human relationship—because they find their origin in God—is a deep reservoir of mystery, never intended to be fully tapped, only to be reverenced and celebrated. This is how the writer Brian Doyle understood it, as experienced on the human plane: "We are utterly open with no one in the end—not mother and father, not wife or husband, not lover, not child, not friend. We open windows to each but we live alone in the house of the heart. Perhaps we must. Perhaps we could not bear to be so naked, for fear of a constantly harrowed heart." At first glance Doyle's observation is a bit bleak; it seems to reflect Carson

McCullers' thinking: "The heart is a lonely hunter with only one desire! To find some lasting comfort in the arms of another's fire." For us, though, loneliness can when transformed (that is, when God comes to us in those moments of isolation or abandonment) become a kind of welcome solitude, where the warm arms that bring us comfort are the Father's, the one in whom the afflicted, wounded human heart often alone finds refuge.

Oh how I wish I could approach every person as Moses did God near Mount Horeb, as one who understood he was standing on holy ground. I would certainly slow down more often, listen better, treat others, particularly those who irritate or aggravate me, with greater patience and generosity. For in us all swirl universes of light and darkness, grace and gravity. (Walt Whitman: "Do I contradict myself? / Very well then I contradict myself, / I am large, I contain multitudes.")

God's hallowed name—from which radiates the light of divine glory—illuminates the divine and the human alike, makes dull things shine and dead things live. The divine name bestows a blessing on us all and transforms every name into a beatitude. On that day when God told Moses God's name, everything changed. It became personal between God and us. We would not see God the same way after that. Nor would we see ourselves and others the same way either, ever again.

The singular, unprecedented encounter Moses had with the divine I AM near Mount Sinai has me thinking now about names generally and the important role names play in helping us carve out our own identities and relationships. (In the parable of the Good Shepherd, for instance, Jesus tells us that the good shepherd knows his sheep, calls them each *by name*. Every time Jesus called someone by name (Zacchaeus in the tree, Mary Magdalene in the garden on Easter morning, Peter on the shore of Galilee during that Easter breakfast, Saul on the way to Damascus, etc.) the summons transformed and healed them. Names matter to Jesus, perhaps because they matter to his Father.

Names have power, so naming (or nicknaming) another is an exercise not entered into blithely. For instance, I, the fifth son, was named William after my father, though my parents gave me a different middle name (Patrick). So not to confuse me and others, I suppose, my family has called me Pat ever since. Still, growing up I felt a deeper kinship with my father since we shared the same first name (and the fact that we were the only lefties in the family). Years later, I concocted an origin story that playfully tweaked my four older brothers' egos. When my father took me into his hands for the first time, I told them, my father raised me up (think: Rafiki showing baby Simba to the animal kingdom in *The Lion King*) and said, "Finally, a son worthy of my name!"

When it came time to choose my confirmation name, I chose Francis. It was a propitious choice because first, Saint Francis was (and still is) my favorite saint, and second, it was my paternal grandfather's first name. And since Patrick was my paternal great-grandfather's first name, I would henceforth become—at least in my own eyes—the physical embodiment of "Hannon." One might think I subsequently began to strut around town more than amble, that my nose began to tilt upward as I neared a sibling. Neither, thankfully, has occurred. My brothers—even after I became a Catholic priest—an ontological change in status you might think would have brought about a shift in their attention—decidedly deferential—still treat me as their kid brother. They keep me humble.

I've only had the privilege of naming two creatures. One was a puppy I found abandoned on my paper route when I was ten. The hapless mutt took one look at me and licked my face. I named him Dr. Zhivago, the eponymous hero of Pasternak's novel. I had seen the movie a few years before (with my grandmother of all people) and had decided it was my favorite film of all time. Of course, I couldn't keep Dr. Zhivago. We kids were bringing strays home just about every day, and we already had a dog and a few cats (as well as a hamster, a guinea pig, and two chickens). My mother brought him to the shelter (where she was on a first-name basis with the employees) a few days later. The other creature I named was a rescue kitten I called Rosa—after Rosa Parks, who played a pivotal role in the Montgomery bus boycott in the early 1960s by refusing to give up her seat in the front of the bus. My kitten grew into a cat with the same independent streak as Mrs. Parks. She didn't take kindly to orders.

A few days ago, I was conversing with an Irish Catholic woman in her eighties. She came from a large family of five older sisters with names like Mary and Rose and Margaret, lovely and popular Irish names. She was named Louise. She told me she hated her name growing up and all through her adult life. So plain sounding, she said, when placed beside the near-lyrical sounds of her sisters' names. But then around three months ago, she told me, she discovered what the word *Louise* means. She smiled. Her blue eyes seemed to sparkle, to come alive as though for too long they had remained dormant, eclipsed by an unwelcome shadow. "It means Famous Warrior," she said.

"Oh," I said, "I so wish you had discovered this sooner!"

"Me, too," she said, "but it's never too late!"

Louise was right. With whatever time she has left on planet Earth, her new identity, stitched into her first name, will open her up widely to wild new adventures. Perhaps she can look back on her life and see that her name has worked to form her secretly, from the day she was first cradled in her mother's arms. In fact, Louise has been a gritty battler her whole life and the gratitude she feels now at having been so beautifully named can work retroactively and wash away completely whatever regret has stained her memory.

Unravel a name and stories spill forth. Stitched into every name—even, especially, God's name—are moments, encounters, surprises, epiphanies, and transfigurations that we bear boldly. In them, we remember fiercely, gratefully, reverently, every tickle and tear, every hidden blessing. As William Blake put it: "Joy and woe /are woven fine, / A clothing for the soul divine, / Under every grief and pine, / Runs a joy with silken twine."

Unravel the name of God and stories of joy and woe pore out as well, like the gentle and glorious sunrise that bathes wide patches of Earth at dawn. Catching such glorious Eden light, our silken souls sing as Mary's did when she met her cousin Elizabeth, who had somehow already heard the news that

Mary would give birth to a boy, the Son of the Most High, and that she would name him "Jesus." Mary's song—linked forever to the sound of her baby's name (Y'shua! Y'shua!)—is ours too. It is called the Magnificat, and it starts: "My soul glorifies the Lord; my spirit rejoices in God my savior."

It's the summer of 1988 and I'm nearing Tulelake, a farming community a few miles from the California-Oregon border. There, on the corner of Highway 139 and Osborne Road sits the Hannon Homestead, seventy acres of rich silty clay loam and a house my paternal grandfather built back in 1932. I'm on State Line Road, not far from a turnoff where back in the spring of 1980 my father, a recently retired lawyer (who had returned to his childhood home) and I, a future priest on spring break, came upon a big pile of county-owned gravel from which we pilfered half a truckbed's worth for the well we were digging next to the house. I smile as I recall the moment Dad thought a highway patrol cruiser was approaching in the far distance. We pealed out like the proper petty criminals we momentarily were.

I am racing there to spend a week on personal retreat at the farmhouse before taking final vows in the Congregation of Holy Cross in August. I'm racing because I want to see my mother, who has been at the farmhouse for a week but who, along with my sister Julie, is going to leave that day to head back to the Bay Area. It will be Mom's last visit to the farm, and she knows it. She has late-stage lung cancer. She stopped chemotherapy treatment a few weeks before, a decision she made that felt less like unconditional surrender and more like a peace brokered in good faith with a foe who had improbably become a good friend. I recall now a conversation we had a year before while we were returning home from Mass on the Feast of All Saints. I asked her if she were afraid of dying. Looking straight ahead, minding the road while her hands gripped the wheel, she said, "Not at all. When I think that someday I get to see your dad again (my father passed in 1985), I get so excited I almost can't wait." It might have been around then that I had begun to understand that the opposite of

66

faith is not doubt but fear. My mother was a deeply faithful Catholic woman, and I like to think that a bit of her graceful and gritty faith rubbed off on me on that evening drive.

I've made the turn onto Highway 139. Off in the far distance is a hump of a mountain locals named "Castle Rock" decades ago. To my left and right are fields of grain, and potato, alfalfa, onion and horse-radish crops in various shades of green. My window is down and I take in the aroma of rich soil and sun-drenched fields like a blessing. Up the road ahead, maybe a quarter of a mile, I see a car approaching. It's sleek and slender and, as it gets closer, I see it is the same cerulean blue of my mother's car. We pass quickly, but not so fast that I don't recognize my sister behind the wheel and my mother in the front passenger seat. Freeze frame: my mother appears shrunken, worn and tired, Yoda-like. Her eyes are closed and her arms are crossed against her chest as though she is cold. I look into my rearview mirror and see her car moving away from me at a steady clip that saddens me. We're on the same road but moving in opposite directions.

I arrive at the farmhouse and, sure enough, her car is not there. I walk in through the back door that leads into the kitchen, and once again I take in two lungs full of air. The aroma of inexpensive coffee (my paternal grandmother and mother were Maxwell House caffeholics), one I have grown to love over the decades precisely because it is one of my earliest olfactory memories, greets me like an old friend. Everything—utensils, dishes, appliances—is as it should be: clean and in its proper place. My mother never left a kitchen without cleaning it thoroughly. (When she tired of reminding us kids to make our beds and put our clothes away and actually run a vacuum across our bedroom carpets a few times a year—in other words, to make the decision *not* to live in a "pigsty"—she would simply shut our bedroom doors slowly and walk away.)

There on the kitchen table is a note written in my mother's elegant Palmer Method handwriting, one I had come to admire for its elegance (*and* forged as a kid when circumstances required it). "Sorry I missed you. Love, Mom," it says. I fold it and put it into my pocket.

I walk around, becoming familiar once again with the beating heart of the place. I am alone, of course, but I feel surrounded, no, *embraced*, by what I can only describe as a warm, quilty spirit. There is the tiny bedroom off the kitchen where my grandparents, my dad, and his two brothers slept for a few winter months in 1932 before my grandfather added on another bedroom that spring, along with a living room and a bathroom, which replaced the outhouse. In the living room: Dad's old Magnavox TV that gets only three channels; the stone fireplace above which rests framed family photographs; the matching cherry wood dining room table and buffet that adorned our old house down in the Bay Area when we were kids. The long couch (there's a picture somewhere of all nine of us kids scrunched together on that couch) reupholstered years ago in a deep burgundy red fabric but now a bit frayed and tired but still usable.

I go into my mother's bedroom last. There is the matching bed and dresser dated from the mid-1800s, brought over from County Cork, Ireland, by my great-great-granduncle Richard Kingston.

My father had died on that bed from a heart attack three years earlier. On the wall above the dresser are framed high school graduation photographs of all us kids. Our broad smiles betray a bit of swagger, I suppose, as we were ready to leap happily but for the most part blindly into adulthood. I sit on the bed and look out of the bedroom window and onto the potato fields across the road. Life—farmers on tractors, farm hands repairing tools, children in classrooms at the school close to the fairgrounds bent over schoolbooks, all those folks out there in the patch of the world I can see buying and selling and mending and eating and laughing and sighing and doing those hundred mundane tasks that make up a day—all of this *life,* unfolding as it should. That moment reminds me now of the beginning of Virginia Woolf's essay, "The Death of the Moth": "It was a pleasant morning, mid-September, mild, benignant, yet with a keener breath than that of the summer months. The plough was already scoring the field opposite the window, and where the share had been, the earth was pressed flat and gleamed with moisture."

I am filled to the brim in a moment, a heartbeat. The farmhouse has become like a Navajo hogan, another *axis mundi*, a cosmic center, a place where Heaven and Earth meet in a kind of sacred hug. In my imagination I see energy pulsating outward, creating waves of hope and gratitude, because in that moment I feel the reassuring hand of God on my shoulder, essentially telling me that I am going to be okay, that my mother is going to be okay, that we—God and I—will spend some quiet time together over the next week and that I have nothing to be afraid of.

Later that day, around sunset, I am sitting on the front porch and taking in the almost bluesy chorus of cicadas along with the cool evening breeze that rustles the leaves of the Cottonwoods nearby. A car or truck races past me occasionally on Highway 139, on its way to Burney to the south or Klamath Falls to the north and to towns in between and beyond, to homes and hearths and families, I hope. My mother and sister are back home in San Jose, I surmise, sitting down for dinner. My brother John will surprise me later in the week with a visit and several bottles of amazing wine.

But for now I am content to raise my pint of beer in a toast to God, my Father, for all good gifts, even the ones that don't appear to me as gifts at first, such as sadness or regret or missed opportunities. All roads, our faith tells us, lead back to God. No two of us—if we have but a lick of hope in us—are ever traveling in opposite directions. And, in this truth, the Father's name is hallowed.

QUESTIONS FOR REFLECTION AND DISCUSSION

1. List some of the favorite names (of people, dogs, anything else) that you have ever heard. How did they touch your soul so strongly? Why do you "hallow" those names?

2. Tell the story of how you got your full name, all the parts of it. What is it about your name that makes you proud? What gives you pause?

3. How can we give a name to an entity whose ways, as the prophet Isaiah wrote, "are so far above our ways." Why do you think Jesus called (and taught us to call) God "Abba" or "Daddy"?

IV

RUINED, THANKFULLY

We must learn to reawaken and
keep ourselves awake,
not by mechanical aids, but by an
infinite expectation of the dawn.

Henry David Thoreau, *Walden*

Few ideas captured the imagination of Jesus more than what he called in the Our Father the "coming" of the Kingdom (or Reign) of God. Aware of the hopeful visions of the prophet Daniel, who saw God's strong arm defeating all the powerful kingdoms on Earth and bringing full restoration to the people of Israel ("But eventually the holy people of the High God will be given the kingdom and have it ever after—yes, forever and ever"), Jesus understood and embraced the mission God entrusted to him.

Jesus clearly felt he was inaugurating, by his ministry of healing, by the power of his cross, and by the glory of the resurrection, a new and everlasting kingdom, akin to the one that already existed in Heaven. His world was of an entirely new order, one rooted in justice and peace, one which the lost and lowly—long imprisoned by fear, addled by oppression of one sort or another, and often hamstrung by despair—could embrace with the gritty hope of the author of Psalm 90 (from *The Message* Bible translation):

> God, it seems you've been our home forever;
>> long before the mountains were born,

Long before you brought Earth itself to birth,
    From "once upon a time" to "kingdom
    come"—you are God.
We live for seventy years or so
    (with luck we might make it to eighty),
And what do we have to show for it? Trouble.
    Toil and trouble and a marker in the
    graveyard.

Jesus came to illuminate a realm that is beyond the earthy grave, beyond sadness and sorrow, but still in the here and now. Seeds of joy and happiness planted in the soil of a suffering would, he promised, blossom into an eternal spring in our lives. He said that the Kingdom of God on Earth has already begun, that it is within us, that all we need do is believe in it and act accordingly. Why else would he have chosen the wildly upbeat prophecy of Isaiah to preach his first "homily" in the synagogue in his home village of Nazareth as told in the Gospel of Luke:

When Jesus stood up to read, he was handed the scroll of the prophet Isaiah. Unrolling the scroll, he found the place where it was written, "God's Spirit is on me; he's chosen me to preach the Message of good news to the poor, sent me to announce pardon to prisoners and recovery of sight to the blind, to set the burdened and battered free, to announce, 'This is God's year to act!'" He rolled up the scroll, handed it back to the assistant, and sat down. Every eye in the place was on him, intent. Then he started in, "You've just heard Scripture make history. It came true just now in this place."

By my reckoning, no poet or prophet has captured the vision of the kingdom of God as Isaiah has done: The Father's infinite *being* is always linked to the Father's *doing*. (We might remember here that in the Spanish translation of the prologue to the Gospel of John, "In the beginning was the Word," we read: *Al principio fue el verbo,* "In the beginning was the verb." The Lord is all action!

Eternal and unconditional divine love pulls us from the depth of whatever darkness we might find ourselves in and bathes us in its liberating light. Poet

Jane Kenyon put it this way: "Let evening come. / Let it come, as it will, and don't / be afraid. God does not leave us / comfortless, so let evening come." It's worth, then, hearing God's voice in all its splendor in Isaiah 65. To me, it's like mouth-to-mouth resuscitation:

"Pay close attention now: I'm creating new heavens and a new earth. All the earlier troubles, chaos, and pain are things of the past, to be forgotten. Look ahead with joy. Anticipate what I'm creating: I'll create Jerusalem as sheer joy, create my people as pure delight. I'll take joy in Jerusalem, take delight in my people: no more sounds of weeping in the city, no cries of anguish; no more babies dying in the cradle, or old people who don't enjoy a full lifetime; one-hundredth birthdays will be considered normal—anything less will seem like a cheat. They'll build houses and move in. They'll plant fields and eat what they grow. No more building a house that some outsider takes over, no more planting fields that some enemy confiscates, For my people will be as long-lived as trees, my chosen ones will have satisfaction in their work. They won't work and have nothing come of it; they won't have children snatched out from under them. For they themselves are plantings blessed by God, with their children and grandchildren likewise God-blessed. Before they call out, I'll answer. Before they've finished speaking, I'll have heard. Wolf and lamb will graze the same meadow, lion and ox eat straw from the same trough, but snakes—they'll get a diet of dirt! Neither animal nor human will hurt or kill anywhere on my Holy Mountain," says God.

"Our Father, who art in Heaven, hallowed be they name, thy kingdom come."

It is to the poor and powerless among us that the kingdom, God's Holy Mountain, belongs. "I'm telling you, once and for all," Jesus says in the Gospel of Matthew, "that unless you return to square one and start over like children, you're not even going to get a look at the Kingdom, let alone get in. Whoever becomes simple and elemental again, like this child, will rank high in God's kingdom." For Jesus, the Kingdom was, and is, about disarming the powerful and unshackling those chained by fear and weariness so that *both* the rich *and* the poor might experience their full humanity as beloved children of God.

In imagining *how* the Kingdom of God would come, Jesus drew upon the everyday experience of his listeners. He likened the Kingdom of God to: a sower sowing seed, a man discovering a hidden treasure in a field, a merchant discovering a pearl of great price, seed planted into soil, a mustard seed, and leaven. I see a unifying thread running through these mini-stories: a sense of wonder, of surprise at stumbling upon a new reality, a disarming truth hiding in plain sight.

With the same sacramental eyes that allow us to glimpse Christ present in blessed bread (poet Patrick Kavanagh: "O Christ, that is what you have done for us: / In a crumb of bread the whole mystery is"), we witness the reign of God breaking forth in our world in ways and places and times that always awaken us from our sleepy complacency, that shock our conventional sensibilities and get us to see the world, already soaked in grace, in a way that, thankfully, intends to *ruin* us from thinking we don't matter. At the very least, the coming Kingdom ought to keep us up sometimes late at night, wondering what it will ask of us when we awake the next morning.

These epiphanies have a way of doing what Irish humorist Finley Peter Dunne said journalism is supposed to do: they "comfort th' afflicted, afflict th' comfortable." Thus we can understand why we are so drawn to the unfolding dramas of hope as we conceive them abstractly *and* resistant to those same stories as they may unfold in our personal lives. Perhaps the conundrum is best captured by Catholic writer Flannery O'Connor when she said, "All human nature vigorously resists grace because grace changes us and the change is painful." In moments of ineffable suffering, we cry out, "Come, Lord Jesus, save me from a meaningless existence!" In our cozy beds, however, we often say, "Um, not yet."

In chapter two of James Joyce's *A Portrait of the Artist as a Young Man,* the teenage protagonist, young and spiritually precocious Stephen Daedalus, is searching for truth and beauty in a world and a Church that often befuddle him. We sense in Stephen's consciousness an inchoate sense that the sexual and the spiritual are two sides of the same incarnational coin; thus his imagined desire for beautiful Mercedes, the heroine of Alexander Dumas' novel *The Count of Monte Cristo* (which he has been reading) can be understood as a desire, ultimately, for God or perhaps for the reign of God in our lives. In his imagination, Stephen sees how his encounter with his beloved would play out:

> He would meet quietly as if they had known each other and had made their tryst, perhaps at one of the gates or in some more secret place. They would be alone, surrounded by darkness and silence: and in that moment of supreme tenderness he would be transfigured. He would fade into something impalpable under her eyes and then in a moment he would be transfigured. Weakness and timidity and inexperience would fall from him in that magic moment.

I don't know about you, but I long for the day when my weakness and timidity and willful inexperience will give way, finally, to a kind of ridiculous courage that will allow me to welcome the Reign of God in some lasting and meaningful way. I put words to this desire every time I pray "thy kingdom come!" It means, though, embracing my fundamental human poverty, such that I will see myself *as I am* in the piercing, shattering, and ultimately liberating light of the Christ who comes to us, as Mother Teresa put it, often in the most distressing of disguises. She also said, "If I look at the mass [of people], I will never act. If I look at one, I will." The likes of Mother Teresa, those grouchy saints who want *us* to learn from *their* mistakes, seem to take us by the chin and, with the Reign of God in sight, direct our faces toward the vagrant, discarded, invisible soul who is right in front of us, trying to establish eye contact with us. We pray "thy kingdom come" with the desperation of the hapless who are walking around with only one shoe on. We shake the heavens with the guttural cry of the mother who cradles her dying baby. We see our salvation wrapped up in theirs.

We see (and can only see) the Kingdom of God as it takes on flesh and bone and blood in the person we see before us, as the startling, earthshaking, my-life-will-never-be-the-same revelation it is always meant to be.

Long before I joined the ranks of the working class as a paperboy, I was a lookout. I recall one afternoon when my oldest brother, Brian, perhaps eleven years old, had me stand on top of the toilet tank in our upstairs bathroom that stood below an open window and keep my eye trained on the street below and report any Mom sightings. I couldn't have been five yet—a tiny boy with the visual acuity of a wary gazelle—but apparently my brother saw something potentially conspiratorial in me. I don't remember what he was up to, but clearly it was no good. Still, I took my job seriously. I saw it almost as a promotion, a reason to believe that I had something of actual value to offer the family.

We Christians are men and women, weary and worn down a bit, or a lot perhaps, with hope to bring. We are the ones—we gritty lookouts—who get to stand by those who are, perhaps, more tired and weary than we and tell them in their dark hour, "Hold on, for see, the Lord is coming." We wait with quickening hearts for the One who comes to set us free.

We have all been drafted by Jesus into his ragtag army of holy hope-catchers. We have been enlisted not just as lovers and dreamers, but also as lookouts—we happy insomniacs who take it as our special charge to scan the horizon at 3:00 in the morning, peer into the faintly erupting dawn, and look for any sign, any hint, any vibration of a galloping God.

I rather like the idea that part of our job description as disciples of Jesus Christ is to—in a way—stand by the bathroom window and keep an eye out for Mom. The boy that lives in me still hopes this is so. Nothing to me back then seemed as important—not Jell-O pudding, my cat Tiger (who gave birth to her litter of kittens on my bed), or the tree fort I would build a few summers later with Boober and J.P., my friends down the street. Sometimes I would look out that upstairs window, on my own time, for fifteen, twenty minutes, just to see if something or someone (a flitting sparrow, a shooting star, a silver coin leaning sideways in a gutter, a skipping girl, a weeping boy—the possibilities are endless) might startle or haunt or delight me into a more thrilling, deeper dimension of living.

I don't remember if my mother ever became aware of the fragile conspiracies we kids scaffolded around her comings and goings. I don't know if she ever knew how often I kept a lookout for her, lest she arrive and find us doing something astonishingly stupid or at least incredibly ill-advised. But if she did, however, I bet she would have been secretly impressed.

QUESTIONS FOR REFLECTION AND DISCUSSION

1. Have you ever been a lookout? If so, tell the story. If not, make one up. Start with what "coming" you were waiting for.

2. Joseph of Arimathea, who took Jesus' body down from the cross and laid him in his own

tomb, was described as a man who was "waiting for the kingdom of God." Some people call this a desire for a "calling" or a "mission worthy of your life." What are you waiting for *now,* at this point in *your* life? If you don't know, how are you going to find out or decide?

3. Why or how is the "Kingdom of God" good news for the poor or powerless? How about for the middle-class or rich? Give examples of each from your own experience.

V

SUCH DIZZY
NATURAL HAPPINESS

I might never again know such
dizzy natural happiness.

Theodore Friend, *Indonesia Diaries*

SUCH DIZZY NATURAL HAPPINESS

I recall a young man I knew for just a short while back in the early 1990s. I was a young priest and the rector of a residence hall at the University of Portland. He was a first-year student from Hawaii. We saw a fair amount of each other in the first weeks of the semester, bumping into each other in the hall or around campus. Mostly he looked lost, not like a wet dog you see every so often—shivering, collarless, cowering in some alley—but pretty close as he tried to negotiate the transition from home to college. Perhaps it was the way his slight shoulders seemed to slump when he walked, as though he were carrying something burdensome on his back, the way an old farm woman used to carry heavy water buckets from a faraway well, strapped to a long piece of wood that lay tenuously across her shoulders.

I knew the look. I had spent a healthy portion of *my* first semester as a freshman at the University of Portland feeling deeply homesick. I can only describe it as a kind of grieving. Something, someone—my younger, naive self; my carefree childhood?—had died. Now unmoored, I was it seemed facing the heavy headwinds of an indifferent and unfamiliar world on my own. Mostly I remember the late night walks I took alone on the Bluff, the acre of campus grass that overlooks the Willamette River below and downtown Portland a few miles away as the crow flies. Often, I sobbed. Where did such suffering come from, this gnawing of the soul? I recall now a brief encounter I had one rainy Saturday afternoon that semester with an old lady in downtown Portland. I had arrived too late to catch a movie and was walking the streets by myself. I must have appeared desolate, a face with hound-dog eyes, for she walked right up to me, and put her hands on my shoulders. Our eyes met. "Hey," she said. "Buck up, little camper." And then she walked away.

I remembered the oddly kind and solicitous letters my older brother Mike began sending home during his first semester away at college. Apparently, he missed us terribly. He all but begged us to write him back. I still remember my mother writing him a letter and asking me for some of the lyrics of Elton John's *Crocodile Rock,* a song Mike loved. I didn't pay his letters much mind then, since I had other matters to concern myself with, namely, trying to survive my first year in high school.

But when I went off to college, they suddenly made sense. The Mike I had grown up with—the one whose *raison d'etre*, seemingly, was to toughen me up, sharpen my wits, speed up my reaction time to unwanted jabs and punches—was no more. Out of his struggle to endure those personally hellish first months of college had emerged a kinder man, one perhaps more attuned to the sufferings of others because he now knew something of soul-ache himself.

The Hawaiian boy came to me one evening in the third week. He sat across from me, his hands resting calmly on his knees. He told me that he was going home the next morning. "A quick weekend trip?" I asked. He paused a beat, allowing the ridiculousness of my response to slink away. "No," he said in a tone that suggested he was disappointed in me for having to spell it out. "I'm going home for good." Being away from home was simply too hard, he said. He missed his family, his friends, his own bed. He would be transferring to a college near home. He simply wanted to let me know. He wasn't asking for advice.

We talked for a while more. Without sharing anything personal, I said, "I *think* I understand something of what you're feeling." (I had called home one night my first semester of college and told my mother I had decided to come home, and she told me I couldn't. She told me she had made my bedroom into her sewing room; that was a lie, I told her, and we both knew it, which made both of us laugh, which saved me.)

I encouraged the young man to stick it out, that things would get better. I told him that by my reckoning (what did I know?) two thirds of life is mostly sticking things out, but we stick them out for that portion of life that is dewy with joy and seeded with peace and wild gratitude and…you get the picture. Over thirty years later, I think I got it about right that night. Mostly, life is *hard*. It means getting up more days than we're willing to admit and facing a pitcher who's got the meanest splitter you've ever seen and a stone face, and cold, hostile eyes. The fact that we're willing to give life our best shot, to me, means everything.

It's why I, along with the hundreds of other adolescent boys in the movie theatre that day back when I was sixteen, jumped to our feet and started going wild when scrappy boxer Rocky Balboa got up one more time from the canvas late in the match, bloodied to a human pulp by one punishing blow after another by world champ Apollo Creed, even though Rocky's trainer was telling him, "Down, down, stay down!" Somehow, Rocky got up. Honestly, I thought I was being transported to some alternate universe that afternoon when I saw him gesture to Apollo Creed with his boxing gloved hands. "Come on," he said, in a Philly accent I can still hear, to his incredulous opponent. "Come on!" I might be overstating how seminal that moment was in my young life, but it feels now as though I were feeling then a kind of electric hope pulsating through my body. As Christopher Friend experienced in his magnificent memoir, *Indonesian Destinies,* when he first saw the rice terraces of Sulawesi, "I might never again know such dizzy natural happiness."

Well, the boy from Hawaii listened to me respectfully and said he would think about it. He shook my hand and said good night. I asked him to say goodbye to me the next morning if he was going home, and he nodded. But he didn't, which was fine. I'm not sure I would have if I had been in his place. You wouldn't have been able to get me on that plane home fast enough. I remember asking God to take care of him, which now seems a bit silly since *of course* God would take care of him. I had nothing to worry about.

Recall in the Gospel of Luke the moment when it seemed the disciples' commitment to Jesus and to the reign of God he was inaugurating might have been wavering. (Earlier Jesus made it clear what he expected: "Anyone who intends to come with me has to let me lead. You're not in the driver's seat—I am. Don't run from suffering; embrace it. Follow me and I'll show you how. Self-help is no help at all. Self-sacrifice is the way, my way, to finding yourself, your true self.") Jesus bucked them up with these words: "Don't be afraid of missing out. You're my dearest friends! The Father wants to give you the very kingdom itself." Another translation says, "Do not worry, little flock, it pleases the Father to give you the Kingdom."

This has always been the will of God on Earth as it is in Heaven: to invite us continuously into the community of love that the Father, the Son, and the Holy

Spirit enjoy eternally, a relationship marked by *agape*, the divine love expressed in complete self-sacrifice and self-gift, without which human love, which draws its energy from this divine love, is not possible. We all know what that "kind of love" feels like, the moment when, astonishingly, we feel so deeply *ourselves*, when we have, for one blessed moment, *lost* ourselves in love, a moment marked by ego-shattering gratitude.

The boy from Hawaii got off the plane in Honolulu later that Saturday and ran into the arms of his parents, who embraced him, I hope, with tears that matched his own: tears of suffering eased and gratitude reborn. He was also certainly running into the arms of God. Was it God's will that the young man suffer? Of course not. Such is the currency of the human predicament. None of us get to leave the planet without our hearts being broken more than a few times, our souls numbed occasionally, our bodies wounded by illness or weathered by time. Did I wish then that the young man had made a different choice? No, it was his decision to make. But even as every choice, big or small, alters the course of any life, God's will remains unchanged. We are all inching our way to the Father, one decision at a time. And God, who sees the seemingly infinite number of possible journeys we all are afforded by human freedom, journeys with us.

All are blessed paths, even the ones that take us to desolate, desperate places. "Even when the way goes through Death Valley," Psalm 23 reminds us, "I'm not afraid when you walk at my side. Your trusty shepherd's crook makes me feel secure." They all lead back to the Father.

"Our Father, who art in Heaven, hallowed be thy name. Thy kingdom come; thy will be done on Earth as it is in Heaven."

A priest friend of mine told me of an encounter he had with a parishioner—a middle-aged woman—a few years ago. They were having a conversation after Mass. It must have touched upon personal and spiritual matters, because at one point she said to him, "Father, do you know what kind of woman I want to be?" "No," he said, "what kind of woman do you want to be?" And she said, "I want to be the kind of woman that when I wake up in the morning and plant my feet on the ground, I hear the devil say, 'O crap, she's up.'"

This is my theory: When you take out all the true narcissists and sociopaths from the human race, the rest of us are exactly like that woman. Every morning we get out of bed as though we have risen from the dead and are to some degree prepared to confound the prince of darkness. And it doesn't matter *how* we awake: groggy, bone-tired, head-achy, or still a little dreamy with a satisfied smile blessed by a deeply enjoyable stretch as though we stepped out of one of those coffee or mattress commercials. Either way we are, on the level of story, the flawed heroes of an often-confounding drama we have named "My Life." And whatever happens that day, we want to be able to pray as we rest our heads back onto our pillows that night, "Lord, I tried," although sometimes it might sound more like an unaddressed sigh, "Lord I tried!"

My informal polling confirms this: None of us, I suspect, got out of bed this morning saying, "Eeeee-excellent! I can't wait to start sinning!" We know how difficult it can be sometimes to make good choices, to become, day to day, often painfully slowly, the kind of person we each hope we can be. It takes weeble-wobbles tenacity to get up every morning and say, in so many words, "Today I'm going to give all glory and praise to God; I'm going to go into the world and give it my best shot, believing that though I may be only one tiny flame on the tip of a tiny candle, even that little flicker of a flame can shatter the deepest darkness." To say this, to believe this, takes guts. The fact that we fail at it many more times than we succeed takes nothing away from the fact that we each have a moral compass that is always pointing us in the direction of the One, True God, whom we dare to call "Abba."

Saint Paul had to come to terms with his propensity for failure in the moral universe. "For if I know the law but still can't keep it," he wrote to the church in Romans 7:15, "and if the power of sin within me keeps sabotaging my best intentions, I obviously need help! I realize that I don't have what it takes. I can will it, but I can't do it. I decide to do good, but I don't really do it; I decide not to do bad, but then I do it anyway."

Paul was at the end of his rope. And then he came to a crucial insight, which, if I'm honest, has salved many a wound in my own struggle to be a good man: "The answer, thank God," he continued, "is that Jesus Christ can and does. He acted to set things right in this life of contradictions where I want to serve God with all my heart and mind but am pulled by the influence of sin to do something totally different."

By Christ's suffering, death, and resurrection, the logic of sin has been destroyed. We walk by Easter light now, and in that light we see who we are and perhaps more importantly, *whose* we are. We are the Lord's. It is his love that we surrender to when we feel utterly defeated, a mercy so strong that we can even be grateful to God for the sin that has reminded us— we serial amnesiacs and often unreliable witnesses to our own behavior—how much we need God in our lives. O happy fault, indeed. Maybe a story might explain what I'm talking about.

SUCH DIZZY NATURAL HAPPINESS

I live in one of our residence halls at the University Portland, and at a hall Mass a few years ago, during the faith-sharing portion after the homily, all of us gathered there were ruminating on the first reading of that day from the Acts of the Apostles and how Saint Stephen, in the face of hostility and recrimination and impending martyrdom, could be so sanguine, so seemingly unaffected by the looming darkness enfolding him. Acts tells us that right before his detractors began to pick up rocks to stone him, Stephen's face appeared to be that of an angel. What faith he must have had, one student in the back said. He had guts, said another. A number of heads nodded. Indeed, I thought, the likes of all those holy men and women who threw their lot in with Jesus back then—they had amazing faith. So we sat there—in studied silence—transfixed for a moment. We were, I suppose, trying to wrap our minds around such a remarkable idea: a faith stronger than fear, stronger than death.

Then, one of the seniors in attendance spoke up. I'm going to paraphrase. You know, he said, I think I know a little about how Stephen must have felt.

Tomorrow, he said, I have a final exam that's going to kick my butt, but you know what? I've got faith! he said. A few around him chuckled. Probably too much faith, he said. At this admission, any number of the students in the chapel that night laughed warmly and knowingly. The senior continued: Yes, he said, I've got so much faith right now, my *faith* has faith! We all broke out in applause. For some good reason, this senior—in a moment when he might have despaired—knew he was not alone. Good for him, I thought. A hope stronger than fear. Emily Dickenson put it this way: "Hope is the thing with feathers / That perches in the soul / And sings the tune without the words / And never stops at all."

Recognizing the power of every good gift given to us—the gift of a daring intellect and audacious will and a compassionate heart, the gift of arms linked in solidarity and imaginations that can see beyond the fog and smoke of human complacency and indifference, the gift of sweat and tears and laughter poured out as healing waters in parched places—beyond all these gifts, perhaps the greatest gift we offer the world is this "soulful thing with feathers" that sings a song that will last forever. And in this cornucopia of gifts, we see reflected God's will for us: that we become the persons we always hoped we could be and, in the fullness of that identity, find our greatest joy and happiness.

The other day while on a walk, I listened to a podcast that replayed a StoryCorps episode from March 1993. In it, I was introduced to LeAlan Jones, thirteen, and Lloyd Newman, fourteen, who collaborated with public radio producer David Isay to create the radio documentary *Ghetto Life 101*, their audio diaries of life on Chicago's South Side. They recorded their comings and goings over ten days, taking us on a bus ride to downtown, to an overpass where they threw rocks at passing cars, to school, to their homes where they interviewed family members. On the second podcast, LeAlan introduced his grandmother, who slept across the hall from his family and kept an eye on them all. (LeAlan's mom suffered from a mental illness, so his grandmother had custody of the children.)

Compared to other people who lived in this neighborhood, LeAlan's grandmother said, she had it easy. "I think I been blessed," she said, "because things could have been a whole lot worse than they have been." LeAlan then spoke. "But Grandma has had plenty of troubles—the kinds of things you see in every family around here. She had one son who was murdered. She has another son who's addicted to drugs and is in and out of jail. Her grandson, my cousin, came down with leukemia when he was six. He was cured, but the medication left him learning-disabled. It upset his mother so much that she started drinking. Now he lives here with my grandmother—sleeps in her bed."

I have met and loved people like LeAlan's grandmother (and LeAlan and Lloyd for that matter, when they're not throwing rocks off of overpasses) my whole life, those who have somehow managed to endure great suffering with a kind of dignity that seems otherworldly. The Chicago poet Carl Sandberg seemed equally mystified by such gritty grace in the first line of his poem titled (ironically, I presume) *Loser*. "If I should pass the tomb of Jonah / I would stop there and sit for awhile; / Because I was swallowed one time deep in the dark / And came out alive after all."

Jonah discovered the hard way (as we all must, I suppose) that God the Father knows where all our hiding places are. We can run, the old saying goes, but we can't hide. Wise holy women like LeAlan's grandmother have learned, I suspect, that we need not run at all, that God's will for all of us is not that we suffer, for God is not a sadist and we are not masochists. God's will for us is that we trust, come what may in a world often indifferent to human suffering, in the Father's parental love that has no human rival.

"Sometimes I think about what might happen to the family if my grandmother dies," LeAlan says on the podcast. "A lot of times I've had dreams that she died—and when I wake up, I run to make sure that she's still there…. My grandmother says she gets her strength to carry on, her wisdom, from the Bible. She loves gospel music. And of all the song she knows, the one she loves the most is called "One day at a time." Lloyd then asks LeAlan's grandmother if she would please sing the song. "With my voice all messed up?" she says. "Do it," he says. "One, two, three."

She does sing. In a leathery voice tempered by age and heartbreak she sings. Her voice is deep and melodious, confident, in pitch. "Do you remember when you walked among men? / Well Jesus you know, if you lookin' below, it's worse now than then. / They're pushing and shoving, they're crowding my mind. / Lord, for my sake, teach me to take one day at a time. / One day at a time, sweet Jesus, that's all I'm asking of you. / So help me today, show me the way, one day at a time."

Lloyd allows for a moment of quiet, as though he and LeAlan have found themselves standing on holy ground. Then he says, "She was hoarse, but she still can blow. Thank you."

I couldn't help but notice that as that segment of the podcast ended, my pace picked up. I almost began to skip. I was heading home, as LeAlan's grandmother was, feeling *blessed*, a word is best translated as "happy."

QUESTIONS FOR REFLECTION AND DISCUSSION

1. "Thy kingdom come" and "thy will be done" are really the same thing, aren't they? (If the Father's will is done, hasn't God's Kingdom come?) Why would the potential coming of that reality cause human beings to "know such dizzy natural happiness"? Give some examples from your life or your imagination.

2. List ten things that make you happy "on Earth." Now put them in order of ultimate importance to you. Then label each "more physical" or "more spiritual"? What does this exercise tell you about yourself?

3. Why do you think Jesus taught us to pray that God's reign come "on Earth as it (already) is in Heaven" in The Lord's Prayer? Give three reasons that might have been why he included this phrase. Then tell a story of how such *hope* works in your life or the life of someone you know.

VI

A LONG, LOVING LOOK AT THE REAL

It is madness to wear ladies' straw hats and velvet hats to church; we should all be wearing crash helmets. Ushers should issue life preservers and signal flares; they should lash us to our pews. For the sleeping God may wake someday and take offense, or the waking God may draw us out to where we can never return.

Annie Dillard, *Teaching a Stone to Talk*

I wonder what the world would be like if none of us, ever, refused an outstretched hand; if everyone gave and gave and gave (often out of their own poverty) with no thought for the morrow; if we Christians took seriously the line in the Lord's Prayer where we ask the Father to give us *our* "daily bread."

While I was living in Berkeley in 2022, trying to write this book, I encountered an older woman—with her wispy white hair and wrinkled countenance she looked to be in her eighties—outside a Safeway. I was on a walk, listening to music through my ear buds when the woman established eye contact with me and asked me something. I plucked my buds out of my ears to find out what she was saying. "I need money to find a place to sleep tonight," she said. "Can you help?"

Now, I had absolutely no reason to believe she was being untruthful about her circumstances, but I was in a hurry (there was a cup of tea waiting for me at Starbucks!) and so I brushed her off as politely as I could and tried to continue my walk. But this female Lazarus-at-the-rich-man's-gate did not take my dismissal well. "What kind of person are you," she shouted, "to walk away from me like this?"

I kept walking.

The woman haunted me for the rest of the day and a good part of the next, which surprised me because I'd had hundreds of such (awkward) requests for alms over my life. I recalled the summer I was in Cuernavaca, Mexico, as a young seminarian learning Spanish. I was walking to Sunday Mass at the cathedral. Just outside the gates to the courtyard that led to the magnificent church's entrance sat a young, tired mother enshawled, a baby on her lap, a mendicant's hand stretched out to me. I'm sure she was in her twenties, but she looked ancient. I had been there less than a week, so my Spanish was spotty at best. I wanted to say, "I am sorry" (*lo siento*—literally, "I feel it"), but in my nervousness I blurted out, *no, gracias*—nearly literally, "No, but thank you for asking." She gave me a quizzical look that still haunts me too, thirty-five years later.

In both of these cases, I was relieved that neither women knew I was a seminarian or a priest.

"Ah, you ran into *her*," a friend told me later that day. Apparently, the old woman I had encountered

on the streets was a regular mid-afternoon occu-
pant of the spot in downtown Berkeley where we
had met—a shadowed, cool refuge from the sun.
She'd been asking for "money for a place to sleep"
there for years. I have to say I was a bit conflicted
now. The middle-class *American* in me—who values
hard work, personal responsibility, fairness, honesty,
etc.—actually resented the woman for making me feel
ashamed at my lack of compassion! (How *dare* she?)
The *Christian* in me—the pray-er of the Our Father—
wanted to kick the crap out of the middle-class American. As Servant-of-God Dorothy Day put it so clearly
in her inimitable way: "The Gospel takes away our
right, forever, to discriminate between the deserving
and undeserving poor."

I would like to report that this particular story
has a happy ending, that I finally had a spiritual awak-
ening and contributed generously to this woman's
in-person Go-Fund-Me request the next time I saw
her. But I can't. A few days later, still smarting from
our first encounter, I ran into her a second time. She
approached me with her eyes again, seeming to have
remembered me.

I stopped. "I need money to find a place to sleep tonight. Can you help?" She was, of course, on script. My soul, in an instant, closed up like a roly-poly pill-bug. I looked at the little cart in front of her, filled with groceries of all sorts. I took a small step toward it, pointed at it, and said, almost like a prosecutor at a trial, "Can I ask you where you prepare all this food? You must already have a place to stay." I had caught her in the act of asking me for help when she obviously did not really need it.

She reacted almost violently. "Don't you *dare* get near my things!" she barked. If she had been holding a cane, I'm sure she would have whapped me with it. I raised my hands as though I were surrendering. (Indeed, in a way, I was defeated.)

Years before I had inadvertently told a young mother at the gates of a cathedral, "No, but thank you," as though she were offering me something I had no need for. Now as I walked away—this time from a surly and offended old woman who had almost *demanded* that I be generous—I had once again, inexplicably, declined the gift she had twice offered me.

"Our Father, who art in Heaven, hallowed be thy name. Thy kingdom come; thy will be done on Earth as it is in Heaven. Give us this day our daily bread."

Jesuit poet Gerard Manley Hopkins put it this way: "Selfyeast of spirit a dull dough sours. I see / The lost are like this, and their scourge to be / As I am mine, their sweating selves, but worse.

Time and again in the one and only prayer he taught us, Jesus comes to us and offers us bread from heaven, whose yeast leavens the soul. In short, he offers us the opportunity to experience a joy the world can never offer: the joy of drawing close to the poor (deserving and undeserving alike) and see in them a brother, a sister; to see in their "scourge, their sweating selves" a way out of the madness of "self-yeast," of self-preservation. In a way, then, such human encounters, which the Our Father constantly prepares us for, can be seen, as theologian Walter Burghardt put it, "a long, loving look at the real." I'm reminded now of the letter Saint James wrote to his

Jewish-Christian community, among whose members must have been a lot of the sorry likes of me:

> Dear friends, do you think you'll get anywhere in this if you learn all the right words but never do anything? Does merely talking about faith indicate that a person really has it? For instance, you come upon an old friend dressed in rags and half-starved and say, "Good morning, friend! Be clothed in Christ! Be filled with the Holy Spirit!" and walk off without providing so much as a coat or a cup of soup—where does that get you? Isn't it obvious that God-talk without God-acts is outrageous nonsense?"

Now, in my clearly lame attempt to defend myself, the old lady outside of Safeway and the mother outside the cathedral were not old friends. And I cannot give alms to everyone who asks for it. I get it. (Although I do know a retired couple in Chicago who give a buck or two to the first person every single day who asks them for money. They joked, "It's the least we can do; we checked!")

I get it. There are issues involved in how we deal as a society with panhandling and with how we deliver social services. In the end, however, what *should* mark us as Christians, like a proud tattoo, if not a kind of "reckless generosity" to anyone who requests coin or compassion?

"Give us this day our daily bread," we say in the Our Father. When we utter this, we are not asking God to provide whatever "we" individually will need to make it through the day but what "we" the members of the human race will demand from our "prodigal Father," who only gives good things. This part of the prayer strikes me now as a scratched vinyl record in which we hear continually "Help me! Help me!" instead of "Help us! Help us!" This petition, indeed the entire text of the Our Father, places a mirror before us so that we might take a "long, loving look" at ourselves and see the face of the poor and the oppressed.

༄

A long, loving look at the real:

- According to the most recent UN statistics, between 720 and 811 million people went to bed hungry on at least some of the days in 2021, roughly ten per cent of humanity.
- Nearly one in three people in the world (2.37 billion) did not have access to adequate food in 2020, an increase of almost 320 million people in one year.
- Globally almost 150 million children under the age of five (22 per cent) suffered from stunting, one indicator of malnutrition.
- In the United States, where according to Feeding America—a nonprofit nationwide network of more than 200 food pantries, soup kitchens, shelters, and other community-based organizations—more than 38 million Americans (one in every nine) and 12 million children (one in every seven) experienced "food insecurity" in 2021. This in a country that, on average,

consumes over twice the minimum daily kilo-calories required for adults. (Only Ireland, per capita, consumes more daily calories!)

Jesus sends the those of us who claim his name and identity as our own into a world of hunger, both physical and spiritual. This is how Luke remembers Jesus' instructions to his disciples, including you and me, in the translation from *The Message* Bible:

> What a huge harvest! On your way! But be careful—this is hazardous work. You're like lambs in a wolf pack. Travel light. Comb and toothbrush and no extra luggage. Don't loiter and make small talk with everyone you meet along the way. When you enter a home, greet the family, "Peace." If your greeting is received, then it's a good place to stay. But if it's not received, take it back and get out. Don't impose yourself. Stay at one home, taking your meals there, for a worker deserves three square meals. Don't move from house to house, looking for the best cook in town. When you enter a town

and are received, eat what they set before you, heal anyone who is sick, and tell them, "God's kingdom is right on your doorstep!"

Every weekday morning Ben would come down from his camp in the West Hills, located a mile or so away from the Downtown Chapel in Portland, and arrive at 8:30 sharp when the metal doors were unlocked and opened. Fr. Dick Berg, the pastor, had put him on the payroll as the church janitor before I arrived that summer in 1995, giving Ben the keys to the basement closet where he would find a broom, a mop and bucket, a squeegee and other cleaning equipment, and get to work.

Ben was a quiet and reserved Hispanic man in his early fifties, mustachioed, standing maybe five-five. His life was a kind of palimpsest, the more immediate memories and details that made up his life story written on old lines long erased. But if you listened carefully, you could hear faint echoes of heavy sighs and sobs that marked moments in his life not easily wiped away or forgotten: combat in Vietnam, drained bottles of beer scattered on the floor like dead soldiers, years of drift and misdirection, lost and broken loves. Sadness didn't seem to haunt Ben so much as accompany him, like two regular travelers on a bus: nod of head, hint of a smile, no words exchanged.

Occasionally Ben and I would chat while he took a break, leaning against the concrete wall of the church that hugged Sixth Street and Burnside. He told me of his tidy camp, tucked away in a quiet patch of Forest Park in the West Hills. He showed me once a worn photo of his baby boy, now a full-grown man, whom he hadn't seen in years. He told me how he solved the intractable problem of inebriates using a side recess of the church, where a back door stood, as a urinal. "I told Father Berg to put a big picture of Our Lady of Guadalupe there and that would do the trick!" he told me. Sure enough, it did. No one, it seemed, had the guts (or the pineal ability) to pee before the Blessed Virgin.

Ben smiled easily now—"after I gave up the booze and returned to church," he said; and it didn't take much to get him to laugh out loud—a pun in Spanish, a salty joke, a quiet off-hand remark. A few steps away from the church, at the corner, stood a water fountain where fresh pure mountain water bubbled up continuously. Everyone who stopped to take a sip or a long slurp knew Ben, it seemed. Lots of pats on the back and shoulder. It was as though he had a gravitational pull to him. Folks wanted to drop into an orbit around him for a while, finding in him a warm and welcome respite from an often cold and indifferent universe.

It was a Friday night and the front doors of the chapel were wide open. Chairs and small tables were already set up in the lobby and on the sidewalk outside. Small lit candles placed on the tables gave our patch of Portland an almost Parisian feel. Several piping-hot pots of hearty soup were set to go, the bread sliced, the day-old pastry from the bakery down the street laid out. A few students from the University of Portland were aproned and ready to serve their guests. The line of the down-and-out waiting to get into dinner for the homeless extended to Broadway, a block away.

A half hour later, the line had finally dwindled to three or four. We were down to maybe three or four more bowls—the ladles already useless, the chefs forced to tip the pot toward each bowl now. Ben appeared finally, the last in line. He got the very last bowl, and it was filled to the brim. He smiled a mischievous smile, like one who takes his good fortune in stride.

Suddenly, around the corner came a boy, no older than sixteen. He looked exhausted. His blue jeans had the patina of grime and dirt on them. His shirt was, shall we say, lived in. I concluded that he had come like so many of the guests before him—a steady trickle of young humanity sopping wet with disorientating fear—from the bus depot a few blocks away and had somehow found his way to the Downtown Chapel.

Ben, holding his own bowl of soup, turned around just as the boy was told he had arrived too late. I don't know if you've ever witnessed a few dozen or so hearts breaking in unison, but they did that night. The guitar player stopped his strumming. Conversations hushed. Honestly, it was my opinion at the time that the angelic hosts and choirs of heaven ceased their hosannas and alleluias and held their breath, and that the Lord God of Hosts peered down from heaven at the drama unfolding on Earth with bemused interest at what might transpire. We all seemed to be reaching for something, anything, we could give the boy. We needn't have worried.

Ben simply said, "Here's your soup, son," and handed the young man his own still-brimming bowl. The boy at first appeared confused. Whatever script he had been following, it did not have such generous lines written. The boy took the bowl as something delicate and sacred and rare; because it was.

So hungry, he immediately began to devour it. By the time anyone noticed, Ben had departed unnoticed. He was already at the Broadway crosswalk, waiting for the light to turn green, when we saw him. I heard one clap. Then another. And another and another. Folks who were sitting stood. The applause for Ben grew in strength. Then the whooping and cheering began, bouncing off the nearby skyscrapers and storefronts like an unloosed kindness.

Feeding the hungry. Giving drink to the thirsty. Visiting the jailed, the lonely, the sick. Why do we perform such "corporal works" of mercy, especially for the stranger? Ben showed us why. And when Mother Theresa was asked this question, she pur- portedly liked to grasp a hand of the questioner, wig- gle one finger of the hand at a time, and say slowly: "You/did/it/to/me." In her saintly mind, anyone could recite the entire Gospel on one hand.

Ben turned around and faced us. He reached out his arms wide, as though he were embracing the world. His grin was spacious, hospitable. He took his left arm and positioned it across his stomach. He took his right arm and tucked it behind his back. And then he bowed. He bowed sincerely, graciously, hum- bly, as a virtuoso on a grand stage. The light turned green. Ben made his way across the street and to the sidewalk that would eventually lead him to Forest Park and his solitary tent and sleeping bag and, we all hoped, a restful night.

I went to bed thinking something big had hap- pened. That I had been a witness to an event that might, if I dared to believe it, come as close as I can get to actually seeing Jesus emerge from the tomb on Easter morning. That if some astrophysicist had been gazing through the giant Magellan Telescope in the mountains of Chile at the moment Ben gave a famished boy some soup, that scientist would have detected evidence of a bright light bending toward Earth by a force stronger than gravity. Stronger, even, than death.

And here is the point of this particular story. We were, all of us at the Downtown Chapel that Friday night in 1995, happy. Repaired. Reknitted. Renewed. Recharged. Not just Ben, nor just the boy who got the last bowl of soup, nor just the other guests, nor just those who cooked or served or cleaned up afterwards. None of us that night were asleep at the switch. We all became witnesses to a gritty hope that can, I suppose at times, touch the edge of despair but without surrendering to it. I can scarcely imagine the ripples of hope that disturbed the space-time continuum that night. Waves and waves of poppling grace, like the echo of cheering acclamation, urging us to action. Just like we pray for in the Our Father.

QUESTIONS FOR REFLECTION AND DISCUSSION

1. Have you ever witnessed or experienced the miracle of the feeding of a multitude, not just with food but with hope? If so, describe what happened. If not, then keep your eyes open because it is about to happen again.

2. List ten or more reasons for *not* giving money (even a small amount) to someone who asks you for a handout. Now give ten reasons to *do* so. Which act do you think will make you happier? Why?

3. What are some other words for "Give us this day our daily bread"? For example, "Give us what we all need to sustain us." Write them down, substitute them once in a while when you pray the Our Father, see if they fill you with joy or at least make you happier than you were.

VII

MERCY CLOTHED
IN LIGHT

"Round up the usual suspects."

Captain Louis Renault, from *Casablanca*,
movie script written by Julius and Philip Epstein

SUCH DIZZY NATURAL HAPPINESS

I still remember how one young Holy Cross priest back in my first year in college began his homily one Sunday night at the chapel on campus. "I have never entertained an impure thought," he said. Students around me shifted a bit in the pew. "They have, though, on occasion," he continued, "entertained me." Everyone laughed. To me it was a revelation. Who begins a homily this way? I think it was about then I began to think maybe I could be a priest.

A while ago—toward the end of Lent—my sister Julie called me after having gone to Confession to a middle-aged priest (in the confessional box) in a neighboring parish. Julie—more Catholic than I at times, it seems—was beside herself. What ought to have been a moment of joyful healing had become a kind of coldly administered yes-or-no exam on sin. "He rattled them off from memory; it was clearly important to him," she told me: "Have you murdered anyone? Have you committed adultery? Have you engaged in lesbian activity?" *(What? Did he actually say, "lesbian activity"?)* The priest's questions came, one after another, like slaps across the face to my sister.

Are you kidding, I thought. There Julie was—a former public defender who had encountered with a sober eye daily human brokenness (blackened eyes, arm casts, vacant expressions) and battled on behalf of her already-defeated clients like a fierce warrior—reduced to tears by her attempt to have her minor mistakes and failings forgiven. A few days later, having regained her footing, and having forgiven him, Julie drove back to that church and spoke with the priest, letting him know how hurtful that confession had been and that she would never slip into that dark box in that church again.

Effective and inspiring teachers, coaches, parents, and pastors will tell you that the least effective way to motivate any student, athlete, child, or person in the pew is by fear. They all know that faith in a loving God (or whatever word they use for transcendence) is a more powerful force. It can withstand just about anything that can threaten it: doubt, guilt, shame, anger, loss, disappointment, despair.

Faith's muscles are lean, sinuous, battle-tested. Only in fear, it seems, can faith grow weary and its bones become brittle, its muscles atrophy. The use of fear to motivate behavior is all about control; faith is all about liberation. Those who lead by fear tell us—like careless poker players—what cards they are holding: without exception, they seem to bear deep and untended wounds themselves, are wildly frightened and desperate for something they think they'll never possess: true forgiveness. They are the Javert to our Jean Valjean in Victor Hugo's *Les Miserables*: at once the jailer and the jailed. People cannot forgive others their "trespasses" unless they have experienced their own "trespasses" being forgiven.

How was my sister Julie able to forgive her poor, insensitive priest-shriver? How can people—as the Lord's Prayer teaches us—forgive anybody else's trespass ("a debt" is a better translation) who feel unwelcomed or wound-riddled themselves? I think it's because Julie—like many people I admire and marvel at—understands *precisely* the spiritual calculus of Christian mercy: unforgiveness too often inflicts more damage upon the wounded than to the one who wounds. "As I walked out the door toward the gate that would lead to my freedom," Nelson Mandela wrote when reflecting upon the day he was freed from his Robben Island cell after twenty-seven years of unjust incarceration, "I knew if I didn't leave my bitterness and hatred behind, I'd still be in prison."

Our Father, who art in Heaven, hallowed by thy name. Thy kingdom come; thy will be done on Earth as it is in Heaven. Give us this day our daily bread; and forgive us our trespasses as we forgive those who trespass against us.

ᔕᖾᑐ

Forgiveness—a divine gift, for sure—bridges the distance human sin creates among us humans. Forgiveness alone heals the deepest wounds. It helps to remember that we can only sin against God. We can treat one another and ourselves like crap every day of the week and twice on Sunday, but we don't sin against each other. Such acts of cruelty or indifference disorient us (they result in a kind of spiritual vertigo) and leave us off balance, soul-queasy, precisely because our relationship with God is the foundation of every human relationship. In such moments God weeps for us, as Jesus wept over Jerusalem that Good

Friday. ("If you had only recognized this day," Jesus cried, "and everything that was good for you! But now it's too late.") He knew the people of Jerusalem were in for a heap of suffering that he could not prevent. And then he died on that cross and reversed the spiritual orbit of humanity and destroyed forever the logic of sin. This is another genius line (among all the other genius lines) in the Our Father: Jesus taught us to pray to be forgiven "just as" or "to the extent that" we forgive others.

"Sin," Saint Augustine said, "is believing the lie that you are self-created, self-dependent, and self-sustained." Later, poet John Donne would put it this way: "No [human] is an island, entire of itself; every [one] is a piece of the continent." So tightly entwined, then, are our human relationships with our relationship with God that it is precisely in our hurting others (and ourselves) that it *feels* as though we have hurt God somehow. That our sin has somehow separated us from God. This, we know, is rubbish. To suggest that our sin could have such power over God is simple heresy. God's mercy, which is greater than any sin, transports us in such moments, like wounded soldiers, from the battlefield to the field hospital (this is one of Pope Francis' favorite metaphors for the Church) where we are stitched back together and made whole.

"Forgive us our trespasses as we forgive those who trespass against us." On one level this petition strikes me as rather dangerous and ill-advised. Do I want God to show mercy to me in the same way I at times show mercy to others? Hell no. Sometimes I take way too long to forgive those who have wronged me. But do I *desire* to be more forgiving of others and therefore of myself? Heavens yes.

So on a deeper level, this particular petition, crafted first in the mind of Jesus and then gifted to us, seems to suggest that Jesus believed we humans have it within ourselves to forgive as the Father forgives, that we can imagine a time when we will have finally surrendered to the mercy of God that has no rival. God's mercy is a mercy stronger than misery. I've discovered the hard way, though, that it takes time. Forgiving as Jesus forgave (he was always so patient with the weak; he never humiliated them) will ask everything of me. And maybe that was Jesus' intention all along when he gave us the Our Father.

Occasionally at the beginning of Mass I will welcome the community by saying, "Well, I see all the usual suspects have arrived!" (At least for me it makes praying the Confiteor easier.) Thankfully they mostly chuckle, for they see that I, of course, include myself among the repentant rabble. I look out upon the People of God, whom the Lord has summoned, and am grateful for the community of gutsy believers in forgiveness we call Church.

We Christians find no comfort in sin, no solace in grudges. We long ago left our gift at the altar because we needed first to seek from or give forgiveness to another human. We struggle mightily to be reflections of God's outrageous love. And occasionally, the morning sun casts us all in soft, forgiving, Galilean light that reveals every blessed wart and wrinkle. How did poet Jane Kenyon characterize such moments of humbling grace? "Our calm hearts strike only the hour, and God, as promised, proves to be mercy clothed in light."

I'm not sure exactly when I finally understood the difference between apologizing and asking for forgiveness. I have a vivid memory of a time in college when I hurt a friend, Randy, deeply. He was napping on his bed in his dorm room one Saturday afternoon, and a bunch of us were sitting around laughing and giggling like total shits (his characterization, not mine), at his expense. He had awakened at one point and been listening to us as we cut him with our words. He understood why the others seemed to find enjoyment in reducing him to a ridiculous caricature. They didn't know him particularly well, weren't part of his tight inner circle. But I was. How could have I joined that pack of hyenas as they cruelly picked at his carcass as he supposedly slept?

I hadn't had Randy's back earlier that day. He was my friend. I loved him, yet I had failed him. Here I am reminded that *love* and *loyalty* are interchangeable terms.

Apologizing, saying "I'm sorry," seemed like worthless currency. Randy and I ate our dinners that evening in a quiet corner of the dining hall. We didn't say a word to each other. We made our way back to the dorm by way of the Bluff, the part of campus that juts out over the Willamette River and Swan Island, with its shipyards and dry docks lit up at night like a county fair. We sat on a bench for a while and stared ahead. Finally I said, "Randy, please forgive me." I glanced at him. He seemed to be mulling over my request. His hands shifted inside the kangaroo pocket of his pullover hoodie. He finally looked over at me. He wasn't smiling, nor was he frowning. "Okay," he said. And that was that.

Here's what I've learned, the hard way. Apologizing is a good start. "I'm sorry." It's the verbal bridge we build for the tiny ruptures we create in the normal course of a day on planet Earth. Inadvertently cutting in line at the grocery checkout; stepping on a toe, bumping shoulders with a stranger, dropping a container of popcorn on someone's lap ("Oh, I'm sooooo sorry!" we say in such moments). Creating a minor stir, driving way faster than the posted speed and then getting caught, cussing or spitting just as a mother and child walk past you. Such infractions do, in civil society at least, require some small sign of remorse. But the apologizer is not exposed in such circumstances. We have not given up any control or power to the apologizee. Which is fine. But to ask another for forgiveness for a real offence is to be completely vulnerable. The one you have deeply wounded (a tiny Band-Aid the apology provides will not do) gets to decide. You are at his or her or their mercy.

I can think of only one other human utterance—when spoken for the first time—that can make one feel as defenseless: "I love you."

༄

But what do you do when the one who has wounded you deeply never asks for forgiveness, or doesn't care if you forgive or not? What do you do then?

A number of years ago I was in the basement of a Catholic church in Shepperton, Australia, a small farming community a hundred miles north of Melbourne. A collection of my essays had recently been published and I was giving a series of readings and lectures in various places around New South Wales. A dozen or so parishioners sat in their metal folding chairs in the basement that night, sipping coffee from their Styrofoam cups, listening intently. I was speaking on the subject of mercy. It struck me as a resonant topic, since I reckoned that many of the folks who joined me that night had descended from one of those unlikely Irish who had been plucked from their homes or prison cells centuries ago, shoved onto British penal ships, and sent to the bottom of the world forever so they could no longer try the patience of their English overloads. (Note to self: continue trying to forgive the English for having oppressed your Irish ancestors for eight hundred years.)

I am a Holy Cross priest. Our order's symbol is the cross and anchor, designed in such a way that one cannot tell where the cross (the Christian sign for mercy) ends and the anchor (the Christian symbol for hope) begins. In talks such as the one I gave that evening, I always quote what are for me the most powerful words in our Rule: "We must be men with hope to bring. For there is no failure the Lord's love cannot reverse, no anger he cannot dissolve, no routine he cannot transfigure, no humiliation he cannot exchange for blessing. All is swallowed up in victory.

He has nothing but gifts to offer. It remains for us to find how even the Cross can be borne as a gift." Such was the gist of my talk that night.

At one point I noticed an old man sitting in a far corner away from the circle. His face was deeply creased and brown—as one who had spent most of his life tilling and squinting under the sun. As I was speaking, he crossed his arms, closed his eyes, and pressed his chin to his chest. He appeared to nod off. The hour was up, the last of the coffee was gulped down, and the last cookie eaten. One by one the parishioners thanked me and departed. The old man approached me last. He pushed a chair next to mine and sat down. He etched the bones of his story. Parents came from Ireland. Limerick, he said. My ancestors, too, I said. *Lovely*, he said. Grew up on a farm. My dad did too, I said. *Lovely*, he said. Had five boys, he said. I have five brothers, I said. *Lovely*, he said. One of my boys, he said, was with some friends on an outing back in 1996, he said. Port Arthur, on Tasmania, used to be a penal colony, he said. A fellow came with a gun and shot the place up. Dozens injured. Killed thirty-five people. One was my son, he said. I'm so sorry, I said.

Thanks, he said. *Father, I've forgiven that man,* he said. You know why, he asked. Why, I said. *Because Jesus told me to "Forgive us our trespasses as we forgive those who trespass against us." I hold no ill will. I can't. Jesus told me to forgive, so I forgave the man.*

Looking at the old man, I saw traces of loss etched onto his face. Frown lines, eye lids that seemed to carry unnatural weight. I saw sorrow. But I did not see hate. Or anger. I believed him. It is possible. We have it within ourselves to forgive—to free others of their debt to us—even when the weight of the wild pain and unspeakable loss we carry can never be balanced by all the gold (or revenge) in the world. An old Shepperton farmer taught me this is true.

QUESTIONS FOR REFLECTION AND DISCUSSION

1. Recall and tell your story of forgiveness. Or your story of unforgiveness.
2. What can you do if your request for forgiveness is not—or cannot ever be—forgiven by the one

you harmed? Hint: The answer is in the Lord's Prayer.

3. List other words that are better than "trespass" or "debt." For example, "mistakes" or "failings" or "sins." Try to substitute them in the Our Father and see how they work for you.

VIII

DESERT GRACES

Ever tried. Ever failed. No matter.
Try again. Fail again. Fail better.

Samuel Beckett, *Worstword Ho*

I was twenty years old and had joined a few class-mates from the University of Portland that late spring of 1980—after my sophomore year—helping Father Ned Reidy, one of the local Holy Cross priests relocate to the Coachella Valley of California, a strip of desert fifteen miles wide and forty-five miles long that rests in the shadow of the San Jacinto, Santa Rosa, and Little San Bernardino mountains. He had been assigned to a regional college as their campus minister and thought we students might enjoy a month living and working in Indio, a long stone's throw from the tony winter havens of Palm Springs and Indian Wells and Rancho Mirage.

While Ned was settling into his new ministry and while we waited for our contracted jobs at a grapefruit packing plant to begin, a couple of us spent a week picking green beans with Mexican migrant workers in a field whose lush viridescent rows of vegetation struck me as oddly beautiful. Some plants, we know, thrive in such scorching climes (mangoes, figs, dates), but green beans? The answer might be found in the valley's name, a misspelling of the Spanish word *conchilla* ("little shell")—at one point, tens of thousands of years ago, the valley was part of the Salton Sea, filled with sea creatures of various sizes. Only the smaller shellfish's calcite, time-resistant carapaces remained—long after their fleshy bodies disappeared—for curious kids to discover. Beneath its silty soil, the Coachella Valley is rich with water.

The average high temperature in June in the Valley is 103.6 F. I got my worst sunburn there, working in those beanfields, shirtless. The seasoned Mexican migrant workers, of course, were fully covered, head to toe. They told me and my fellow-gringo Mike to be careful, but we didn't listen. We spent the next several days coating each other's backs with aloe vera gel and sleeping on our stomachs. We encountered a rattlesnake one morning in that beanfield. Couldn't have been more than ten feet from us as it slumbered in the shade of one of the bean plants. One of the workers killed it before it could spring. The guy who killed it brought it home (apparently, he made a delicious stew with it, along with celery, potatoes, carrots...and green beans).

On Saturdays we lay lifeless on the floor of the living room where we were staying, the swamp cooler wheezing like an old man, household fans swiveling every which direction. I remember one afternoon I was in a half-dream state thinking I was getting a glass of water and drinking it. In fact I did grab the glass of cold water that was resting beside me on the carpet. As I said, I thought I was standing, so I placed the glass next to my lips. Mike was watching me.

"You were just layin' there," he said later, laughing so hard I thought he was going to cough up a lung. "You took the glass and just poured it all over your face!" Whatever embarrassment I must have felt dissipated quickly. It felt too *goooood*.

It was kind of a baptism for me, now that I think about it, that watery encounter. For over the next few weeks, I sensed I was being invited, as Jesus had been after his Jordan River encounter with the Baptizer, to the desert where I might be put to the test by God—to begin to test the mettle of my faith, to see if I could face some truths about myself without buckling over.

I've recently concluded, by the way, that God finds—in a good way—some delight in putting us to the test. (God the test-driver: "Let's see what this baby can do on the open road!") God designed us, after all, for greatness. From Psalm 8 in *The Message* Bible: "I look up at your macro-skies, dark and enormous, your handmade sky-jewelry, moon and stars mounted in their settings. Then I look at my micro-self and wonder, why do you bother with us? Why take a second look our way? Yet we've so narrowly missed being gods, bright with Eden's dawn light."

On my better, stronger days, I *want* God to put me to the test for the reason, I think, Jesus intended when he devised this particular intention: It's the only way I will be able to grow as a human, a Christian, a priest. On my weaker days, I cry out to God, "Please don't put me to the test!" The implication here being, I think: "Please don't test me beyond my ability!" Still, as spiritual athletes, we recognize how crucial a role failure plays in our attempt to excel. Failure, of course, never feels good, but it is necessary if we wish to grow into our full humanity. *Deficio ergo sum.* "I fail, therefore I am." And thus I pray.

"Our Father, who art in Heaven, hallowed be thy name. Thy Kingdom come, thy will be done on Earth as it is in Heaven. Give us this day our daily bread and forgive us our trespasses as we forgive those who trespass against us. And lead us not into temptation.

～

"The desert prowls like a lion," the writer Richard Rodriguez once observed. Heat pulses up from the griddle-hot soil. From above, damning sun burns exposed skin layer by layer. Desolation, the color of a blanched skull.

"Somewhere in sands of the desert," Yeats writes in *The Second Coming,* "A shape with lion body and the head of a man, / A gaze blank and pitiless as the sun, / Is moving its slow thighs…."

Then there's Saint Peter's advice in his first letter that is now part of the last prayer the Church utters before going to sleep each night: "Keep a cool head. Stay alert. The Devil is poised to pounce [like a lion] and would like nothing better than to catch you napping." It strikes me now that the desert might be the last place I ever want to find myself, at least alone. Yet, like the beloved Son of God, I—we—are often driven there because bare-boned truths are found there, and only there.

God planted in our embodied souls the desire to be united with the Father, just as the Son is united with the Father. *Living* with that desire can be mighty difficult at times, given that it often seems to compete with other, more earthly desires that can mislead us. The word we use for this in the Lord's Prayer is *temptation*. Even holy desires seek physical expression. Jesus spent those forty days in the testing wilderness so he could discover and celebrate his identity as the beloved Son of God *and* Son of Mary and Joseph. Embracing these seemingly opposing identities—and uniting them ("let heaven and nature sing!")—opened Jesus' eyes to the liberating path before him, a path that would eventually lead him to the Cross and to fulfilling the mission of mercy worthy of his life.

Mike and I moved from beans to grapefruits. Six hours of packing grapefruits into cardboard boxes at a small family-owned grove and packing plant. I got good at it. Since we were being paid by the box (around fifteen cents per), I learned quickly how to arrange the first row of grapefruit so that afterward I could pour the rest of the grapefruit that came down the line and they would naturally adhere to the pattern, row after row. I became so efficient that during the half hour I got to pack the largest grapefruits (we rotated that top spot out of fairness). I was making around fifteen bucks an hour, no small change back then.

One of the seasoned workers, an Hispanic woman in her forties—let's call her Maria—did not like me. As far as she was concerned, it seemed to me, I was just another boy who was, for all intents and purposes, taking money out of her pocket. When Maria was packing behind me, she flung insults at me in whispered Spanish. When it was my time at the front with the huge grapefruits, she watched the clock like a hawk so I didn't enjoy a second more of my allotted time. A few times I went two or three seconds longer and, well, let's just say I learned how to say some of the juiciest swear words in Spanish. I would turn around and look at her. Her ink-black hair, tied tightly into a ponytail that draped her back, completely exposed her tanned face, glistening with daily contempt for me.

I tried to win Maria over with my natural charm (I was charming), my good humor (never biting), my Hannon likeability (life of the party)! Occasionally, I bought her chips and sodas from the vending machine. I unpeeled grapefruits for her during breaks as we all sat in the shade at the loading dock. She'd grab the chips and sodas; she'd bite into the juicy flesh of the grapefruit I handed her and walk away, unsmiling. And then when we were packing boxes again, she'd be waiting to pounce, the prowling lion in her waiting to devour me. I grew to despise her. I'd arrive at six in the morning and she'd be in the lunchroom already taping up her fingers, scowling. She'd look up at me (through me?) for a second, look down at her fingers again, and shake her head, as though I were a great disappointment to her and, by extension, the rest of humanity. If there were a Geiger counter that could have measured my antipathy toward her as I made my way to the refrigerator those mornings, it's rapid clicks would have denoted intense, burning radiation.

A few days before I departed—we University of Portland students had been packing grapefruit for over a month by then—I saw Maria sitting on a bench under a tree near the Catholic church in the neighborhood where I was living. From a distance she appeared to be reading a letter. From fifty or so yards away (I dared not draw closer) I could see she was sobbing. Her shoulders shook. Her belly heaved beneath the cotton fabric of her dress. She was human, after all. She never saw me. The next day, a Monday, she was taping her fingertips again in the lunchroom. Same scowl. Same look of disappointment as she surveyed my countenance. We never spoke again.

I thank God now for that woman, who for some reason did not like me. She became an unwitting participant in my becoming a better human being. However constrained her world was, my world was smaller. The world is, for a twenty-year-old, perhaps always too small, too constricted, too self-focused, too prone to a sticky solipsism. Maria enlarged my world and thus my heart. If Walt Whitman is correct in his poetic self-assessment ("I am large, I contain multitudes"), then he has partly nailed us all. I'll never know why Maria disliked me. She may have had a very good reason, maybe not. But who cares? She was not first person to whittle my ego down to a healthy nub. And there have been dozens since, all instruments of grace in the racing-gloved hands of God.

We can enter the desert, it seems, anywhere: Vast swaths of wilderness—materializing at a moment's notice—mark the borders of loneliness or heartbreak or grief or bone-gnawing desire or any other of the heart's badlands. Where once bucolic pastures extended to some distant hopeful horizon, the desert appears, wide open like a yawn. And we enter it because we believe we will emerge from it more loving, more kind, more forgiving and accepting. In short, we will become more fully ourselves by surrendering ourselves to the desert heat of God's merciful love.

In the spring of 1986, my mother—by my reckoning—took her first airplane trip alone, to visit me at Notre Dame, Indiana. My father had passed away the previous autumn from a heart attack, and Mom came to spend a week with me while I was studying in the seminary. The last time I had seen my parents together was the previous summer when they drove me back to Notre Dame from Colorado, where I had recently taken my first vows in Holy Cross.

Now Mom was alone, a widow and an orphan (her mother had died suddenly, too, from a heart attack three weeks after my father died) taking morning walks around the lakes of Notre Dame as I went to class. She knitted and read in the afternoons as I studied, and we spent an hour each night chatting. We went out to a movie one night—a James Garner flick; my mother *loved* James Garner. Ten minutes into the movie, the screen suddenly went black. We waited around five minutes—my mother, perhaps fifteen other patrons, and I—for it to start up again, and when it didn't I went out to find out what was going on. The lone employee—a teenage boy standing lackadaisically behind the concession counter—grew alarmed when I informed him of what had happened. He raced up to the projection room to discover unspooled film up to his waist, and growing. We got a rain check but never did see that movie together.

I remember being very protective of my mom then. She was a small but strong woman, barely five foot tall. As a boy, I marveled at her arms—well-knit and muscular, the way I suspected farm women's arms were, though she had always been a city girl. But she struck me now as unusually frail, a bit worn out. I noticed she coughed more. We took the South Shore train to Chicago to see the musical *Big River* one Saturday. The big fellow in the ticket booth was a little short and ill-tempered with my mother, and I was ready to verbally pounce on him, but my mother, sensing my rising temper, intervened. "How *are* you this morning?" she asked him. Her arms were folded placidly on the counter, which she could barely reach. She looked at him with her disarming, pale blue eyes and he just melted. "So sorry, Ma'am," he said, as he fumbled with two tickets behind the screen. "Been a rough day already and it's not even nine."

"Oh, haven't we all had days like that, she said. *She still has it,* I thought, *my mother, the moxie, the keen eye for another's quiet suffering.*

A few months later she called to tell me that she had gone to the doctor again for her cough. They had run their tests and discovered she had late-stage lung cancer. They gave her, optimistically, a year to live. She lived for two.

I remember walking with her down the corridor of the oncology ward one evening. She was wearing her duck slippers, a Christmas gift from her children, fluffy cotton things of orange and yellow with cartoonish eyes and duckbills. They made me giggle as we walked down the hallway, past opened doors and sleeping patients. Returning to her room, I wondered aloud if it was okay to laugh as I did. Ah, Pat, she said as she crawled back into bed, "if you stop laughing, you die." I never understood in those days leading up to her death how it was possible for her (or anyone else, for that matter) to remain so hopeful in the face of so much body-breaking suffering.

The Irish rock band U2 came into my view around that time, equidistant from my father's unexpected death and my mother's expected passing. My younger sister Julie alerted me to the band. She had seen them during the second leg of their "Joshua Tree Tour." She told me I *really* needed to listen to that album. She never told me why I needed to, but perhaps she suspected I was struggling as we all waded more deeply into the ebb and flow of the mourning waters.

I listened to the CD one evening in my bedroom back at Notre Dame. The last few lines of the second track on the album, *I Still Haven't Found What I'm Looking For,* struck me: "I believe in the kingdom come / Then all the colors will bleed into one / Bleed into one / But yes I'm still running / You broke the bonds / And you loosed the chains / Carried the cross / Of my shame / Oh my shame / You know I believe it / But I still haven't found what I'm looking for." Bono is joined by a chorus of voices as the last line repeats four more times. *I still haven't found what I'm looking for.* The drumbeat is steady, mimicking a seasoned cross-country harrier's heartbeat; the rhythmic, hurried cadence of the Edge's guitar suggests urgency. Bono's sings in a higher register, giving the lyrics an almost bluesy, gospel music feel.

It reminded me of a lounge singer—an older Black woman with graceful, elegant arms—I encountered once at a blues nightclub on the South Side of

Chicago one summer evening. Cast in soft purple light as she sat on a stool near the piano, she seemed to have emerged from the Harlem Renaissance world that Black writers such as Zora Neale Hurston and, later, James Baldwin created in their fiction. She smiled as she sang. Playful and wise, her voice was. Her Brazilian andalusite skin glistened gloriously, as one who had fought the good fight and kept the faith.

They—Bono and that woman—seemed to be telling me the same story. The narrator of Baldwin's story "Sonny's Blues" put it this way: "Creole began to tell us what the blues were about. They were not about anything very new. He and his boys up there were keeping it new, at the risk of ruin, destruction, madness, and death, in order to find new ways to make us listen. For, while the tale of how we suffer, and how we are delighted, and how we may triumph is never new, it always must be heard. There isn't any other tale to tell, and it's the only light we've got in all this darkness."

The dusky sky that evening in my bedroom was a triumph of light purple and orange and yellow. Twilight tells a hopeful story too, if you listen carefully.

The Golden Dome of the administration building across the lake shimmied. The branches of the trees that stood in soft shadow nearer to me took on an hieratic air, pointing me to a vast, mysterious, and darkening sky. I took a deep breath as the song ended. I felt something seep back into me, like a deep dry aquifer being refilled from some unknown source of pure refreshing water.

I'm not exactly sure when it happened, but one morning I awoke and got out of my seminary bed not believing in God. It was as though I had caught some virus (not unlike Covid, in this analogy) that had, in an instant, taken away my sense of taste and smell, as well as sight and hearing, for anything that hinted of God's presence. It was like I had stepped into the world of Beckett's *Waiting for Godot,* inhabited by Vladimir and Estragon, two friends who are waiting patiently for the mysterious Godot who continually sends word that he will be arriving but never does. I didn't breathe a syllable of this to anyone but my spiritual director who was, thankfully, patient and hopeful *for* me (when I could be neither) while I entertained the very real possibility that my faith in God had died.

Losing one's faith, I would discover, is not a new story at all. In the face of suffering and death—one's own or some else's—faith in a love stronger than death can tilt uneasily to one side and topple. But it was new to me.

Surprisingly, it was not a particularly dark time for me, at first. Interesting, yes. Surreal, for sure. Disorienting, absolutely. But I wouldn't describe those months—almost a year, actually—as frightening or even worrisome. Once I accepted my doubts as normal, it was, in this respect, as though I were a child again, finding the world—now appearing only in tones of film-noir gray—at every turn oddly fascinating.

So my life—such as it was—went on. I attended classes, meals, Mass, community prayer, meetings. I went on bike rides, played racquetball, completed my assigned house chores, went to movies with classmates. I carried on as the Pat Hannon everyone had grown accustomed to. Nothing had changed, yet everything had changed. I was getting a taste of a life that was not in any way, it seemed, affected by the gravitational pull of God. I was floating, as one might in dreams, on air.

Looking back I'm still a bit incredulous at the fact that I was not paralyzed by fear or guilt or shame, as others might be at the thought of being seemingly so willfully indifferent in the face of so great a loss. It would seem that I should have been fighting mightily to keep my faith alive! After all, I was studying and preparing for my life as a Catholic priest. Still, I was my lawyer-father's son. The evidence, as far as I could tell then, was clear: God was no more.

And then one day—close to that one when I was listening to U2—it struck me that I had had enough. It wasn't that I found my gray world unsatisfying or even overly lacking. Part of me then could imagine a future rich in friendship and family, one as soulful and exuberant (and tragic and heartbreaking) as any other. Then it hit me, (was I brushing my teeth at the time? Showering? Praying?) that such a life of atheism or, worse, agnosticism would never be enough for me.

A nascent insight began to emerge: It wasn't plea-sure I was after. Not even happiness. It was, ulti-mately, joy—those rare, sticky encounters with eternal moments, divine wormholes that transport us to wildly unfamiliar places beyond Earth's horizon—that I was after. And it seemed to me that the seeds of such joy, necessarily, must be planted in the soil of suffering, and that it would require great patience. Annie Dillard's insight about how a jewel of a sentence arrives unexpectedly to a patient writer comes close to how this fledgling understanding of God's grace came to me then. "From the corner of your eye you see motion. Something is moving through the air and headed your way," Dillard wrote. "It is a parcel bound in ribbons and bows; it has two white wings. It flies directly at you; you can read your name on it."

I recall the next time I sat with my spiritual direc-tor and told him what had happened. He smiled. Later he hugged me. "Welcome home," he said.

I stood before my bedroom window listening to that U2 song over and over. I closed my eyes and breathed in deeply. I did feel as though I *was* home again. My personal journey of faith has been—and it continues to be—a wild dive into the dark where, at times, I can become lost. Untethered from the center of my existence for a while, I had wandered. I thought I had stopped believing in God, but that was not true. God had been with me the whole time, trusting in me to find my way, not back to a familiar place but to some new place, startling, breathtaking. God, it turns out, is like Ernest Hemingway's Paris of the 1930s: a moveable feast.

The first lyrics of that U2 song go this way: "I have climbed highest mountains / I have run through the fields / Only to be with you / Only to be with you / I have run / I have crawled / I have scaled these city walls / These city walls/ Only to be with you." This is a prayer Jesus could have prayed to the Father as he made his way along Jerusalem's crowded streets that Good Friday, past the city walls and to a hill (God's highest mountain, I believe now) where his cross would be planted like the life-giving tree it became, one on which he would be nailed and where he would cry out, "God, God...my God! Why did you dump me miles from nowhere?"

Lamentations such as Jesus' suggests a faith strong and well-knit as my mother's arms, graceful and elegant as the arms of that Black woman's I saw in that South Side Chicago Blues joint. Jesus' arms, stretched across the patibulum of his cross—dignified, strapping—holds the world still, in all its sorrow and all its joy. Saying yes to the Crucified One every day—even within the sometimes maddening silence of the Father—strikes me now as a daring, gutsy act of faith.

QUESTIONS FOR REFLECTION AND DISCUSSION

1. Have you ever had a crisis of faith? Are you having one now? Describe it. Why is it a "temptation"?
2. What is it about a life of faith in God would you miss the most if you abandoned it? Make a list.
3. What song that you love speaks most to you about the ultimate meaning of life. Look up the lyrics online, print them out, and memorize them. Share them with others.

IX

BIRTH-CRY

Badness cannot succeed even in being bad
in the same way in which goodness is good.
Goodness is, so to speak, itself;
badness is only spoiled goodness.
Evil is a parasite, not an original thing.

C.S. Lewis, *Mere Christianity*

SUCH DIZZY NATURAL HAPPINESS

If there is another universe that has another planet Earth like ours, though lacking in evil, I would not want to live there. That sounds like an awful thing for a priest to say, but my strong suspicion is that I would be bored to tears, the way I am with a story that has no real conflict, tension, shadows. In fact, without tripwires, tawdry affairs, feckless pawns, (seemingly) hopeless detours, betrayals, backstabbings, inoperable tumors, earthquakes, and other gripping encounters with natural disasters (in western jurisprudence we misname them "acts of God") and human mistakes, shortcomings, failure (in western theology we misname them "sins against God), there would *be* no story.

In 2022, I watched the NHL's Colorado Avalanche defeat the Tampa Bay Lightning and win the coveted Stanley Cup. Watching one scruffily bearded, teeth-missing Avalanche player after another take turns hoisting the Cup over their sweaty heads as they skated deliriously happy circles around the rink made me choke up (and they weren't even my team). Their joy—born from much struggle, failure, defeat—was palpable. Without failure there would be no hockey, nor any sport at all, and who'd want to live in a world like that? There'd also be no rock climbers or knitters or potters. No Blues or jazz or rock-n-roll or rap or classical music. No illness. No tears.

Okay, so I can't imagine we'll have need in Heaven for novels and hockey. Or illness or tears, for that matter. In the meantime, however, here on Earth we are to relish our humanness and be grateful for it, even if—or especially because—part of all of us is broken, prone to failure, susceptible to committing a bad act. It bears repeating—except for those whose engines of a conscience, for lack of lug nuts and fuel lines, are not running properly: We humans are supposed to get up every morning ready to bravely face ourselves and the world and make a positive difference. The fact that we fail often at getting it right need not intimidate us. Anger us, sure, for a while. Deflate us, absolutely, for a brief moment. But then comes the good stuff: mercy, forgiveness, the applause, the hugs, the healing laughter, the hoisting of the pint or the baby or the Stanley Cup. Heaven on Earth, as it were. Or certainly hints of what's to come. Those triumphs that make all the struggle worth it.

Our human propensity for failing to do good (and for doing bad) is baked into us, and the sooner we accept that the better off we will be. Let me be clear: I am not suggesting we should be indifferent to sin. The experience of evil (the absence of good, or in many instances a *misdirected* good) must always, leave us feeling, at least for a while, a bit lost, sad, angry, exasperated, furious even. Evil manifests itself in ways that *must* elicit from us an active, loving response. In the face of structural sins of racism, sexism, homophobia and transphobia; hunger and oppression of all kinds; war and environmental destruction; each of us must, if we have a healthy conscience, figure out how to make a difference, how we might, as Dorothy Day put it, "throw our pebble in the pond and be confident that its ever-widening circle will reach around the world."

And we accept the truths of our beautiful and broken humanity. We can be charming and nasty. Grudging and gracious. Miserly and merciful. Some, perhaps, more than others. All of us, as it turns out, would make compelling heroes (complicated, inconsistent, worthy of redemption) of the next great

American novel. And that's a good thing. In this spirit, then, we can see in the last petition of the Our Father, a reflection of ourselves at our most needy—when the weight of our sin, or the weight of humanity's sin—seems too heavy to bear. Liberate us, Father, free us up from the burden of our sin in this moment, so I (we) can love more freely again. This last petition inoculates us from the virus of cynicism. It prevents us from giving up on ourselves, on someone else, on the world, on God.

Our Father, who art in Heaven, hollowed be thy name. Thy kingdom come; thy will be done on Earth as it is in Heaven. Give us this day our daily bread; and forgive us our trespasses as we forgive those who trespass against us. And lead us not into temptation; but deliver us from evil.

For a while now, I've been intrigued by the "little people" (as one scholar characterizes them) in the Gospel of Mark: the hapless and nearly hopeless, who became the mostly nameless cadre of desperate outsiders who would have—had they not stepped bravely out of the deep shadows of their lives and approached Jesus on one particular day—gone to their graves quietly and without fanfare. They, like the poor today, seemed to bear the brunt of evil in the world of their day. They—the leper, the friends of the paralytic of rooftop fame, the woman with the hemorrhage, the poor widow, the women at the cross and later at the tomb, and the Syrophoenician woman—were willing to cash in what little dignity they have left for the chance to be healed by Jesus. He was the first one who could look evil in the face and not blink and could therefore make them whole again or give them the courage to become instruments of healing for someone they loved.

Here I'm reminded of another unnamed person from the Gospel of John (the only place where the story appears): the woman caught in adultery who, save for Jesus' intervention would have been publicly stoned to death. In his recounting of that moment, Saint Augustine wrote, *relicti sunt duo miseria et Misericordia* ("the two of them alone remained: misery and mercy"). The two of them. Only. Alone.

Remained. A miserable woman and mercy in the flesh.

How often have we found ourselves in such dire straits, stripped of pride and any pretension, holding onto one thing only: that surprisingly sturdy string of faith we pray for in the Lord's Prayer that twines us to the sacred heart of Jesus, a faith that promises us that God's mercy will, once again, be stronger than our misery.

I suppose I'm drawn to the Syrophoenician mother whose daughter is deathly ill because she was a realist. She knew how unkind the world could be to women such as her. How if she were stumbled upon, the stumbler would treat her as a stray dog—dismissively and more than slightly annoyed. She knew that in the grand scheme of things she wasn't particularly important. But she also knew something of love, how fierce it can be and how unstoppable it is when someone you love is drenched in misery.

So when Jesus initially rebuffs her—when he says in so many words 'I'm sorry, Ma'am, but it's not your time yet'—she gets it. At the moment, there's a queue and she's got to wait her turn. Nonetheless, her love for her daughter overrides the rules and dictates that she make a holy nuisance of herself. (Even if, should anyone ever hear this story recounted, Jesus himself might be cast in an unflattering light, seen as slightly petulant, a bit too protective of his much needed solitude.)

So this also-unnamed woman pushes back. *Audentis Fortuna iuvat* ("Fortune favors the bold") goes the Latin proverb. But let's be clear. Like all the other little people in Saint Mark's account of the Good News, she knows who Jesus is and what he can do. She has faith in him that must have revived Jesus' spirits—given how exhausting his own disciples (especially Peter) could be with their inability most of the time to understand who Jesus was and why he came into the world.

This woman got Jesus right away. She knew with a faith that almost seems instinctual that he would treat her, eventually, with dignity and respect, that in their single encounter she would be treated as though she were the most important person in the world. This is what happens when our misery meets divine mercy.

I love this nameless mother, because she did not blink in the face of seemingly divine indifference or slink away apologetically. She reminds me that, when I am most impatient with God, when in my momentary misery I cry out in pain purchased by whatever bad act I have done or good act I have not done and am met not with immediate relief but with silence, I need not slink away ashamed for having made a nuisance of myself.

And so, we pray, "Deliver us from evil" at the end of the Our Father. Save us. Pluck us from the quicksand of our sin. In the prayer's embolism, a stentorian echo of that last petition, the priest at Mass prays: "Deliver us, Lord, we pray, from *every* evil [my emphasis], graciously grant peace in our days, that, by the help of your mercy, we may be always free from sin and safe from all distress, as we await the blessed hope and the coming of our Savior, Jesus Christ." That last petition reflects, as does the Our Father as a whole, the eternal horizon in an earthly moment. The power of evil *has* been defeated. It just doesn't know it yet.

And then, along with most of our Protestant brethren, we remind ourselves that "Thine is the Kingdom, and the Power, and the Glory. Now, and forever."

SUCH DIZZY NATURAL HAPPINESS

In the end, evil—sin, human failure—has nothing to offer us except, by the indefatigable grace of God, the good it will lead us to do. Declawed and defanged, the beast is helpless to the love and good will that overshadow it. Gandhi put it this way: "When I despair, I remember that all through history the ways of truth and love have always won. There have been tyrants and murderers, and for a time, they can seem invincible; but in the end, they always fall. Think of it—always."

Eric Hamilton, seventeen years old, died one summer night in 1997 when I was working at a parish near the border of Oakland, California. Someone drove by and shot him while he was sitting on the front stoop of the house where he was staying. And though I read about it in the paper a couple of days later, his story didn't hit home for me until I got a phone call from a young woman named Yvonne, his girlfriend, a week later. Eric had friends, she told me. They wanted to give him a funeral.

Apparently, Eric lived mostly on the streets. On occasion, a friend would take him in for a couple of days, but mostly he was content to live in the 1978 Cutlass he had bought for three hundred bucks from a gas station owner in Jackson, Mississippi, on the day he turned sixteen. Not much later, his stepfather kicked him out of the house after a fight and Eric, probably tired of all the beatings, figured he could better go it alone. He moved to California, for by his reckoning an Oakland alley shined in comparison to the cold comfort his Mississippi home had afforded him. In the six months Eric was homeless, he surrounded himself with a motley crew of ear-pierced and tie-dyed teenagers, who traded personal horror stories like baseball cards. And on a Friday in August, we all gathered at the church to remember him.

They arrived in groups of four and five and huddled together like lost sheep outside the church, puffing on cigarettes, the boys fidgeting with their ties that seemed to hang on their necks like nooses, the girls occasionally adjusting their nylons, which suggested they had recently purchased them at Walgreens or Rite-Aid. They looked somehow older than their years; and they carried themselves with a dignity you might associate with men and women of a higher social rank. They rightly judged the sobriety of the occasion. Eric's nearest relative, an uncle from Oakland, had decided not to hold a funeral service, leaving Eric's young friends to figure out on their own how they might do the work of grief. It was as if an ancient voice had beckoned them to the one place that would welcome them. And so they came.

For most if not all those teenagers, it seemed to have been a long time since they had been in a church. Milling around outside as the bells struck nine that morning, they seemed unsure of the next move. So I went outside and invited them in. They spread out among twenty different pews, keeping the first few rows completely empty. The gospel passage they had chosen came from the Gospel of John, in which Jesus encouraged his disciples not to let their hearts be troubled when he left them. "You trust God, don't you? Trust me," Jesus told them. "There is plenty of room for you in my Father's home. If that weren't so, would I have told you that I'm on my way to get a room ready for you? And if I'm on my way to get your room ready, I'll come back and get you so you can live where I live."

A boy who mostly lived in the back seat of his Olds Cutlass finally had a real home. And we all believed he was going there.

We gathered at the table for Eucharist. If you had been there, you would have shed a tear at the sight. I did. At my invitation, thirty teenagers—hands in pockets or holding onto handkerchiefs—slowly made the trek to the altar, as if it had taken them their whole lives to get there. Their faces, painted in grief and sadness and tinges of anger. Wounds exposed; eyes scanning the world for a tint of hope. They looked like what we all look like when our hearts are broken, when our exposed wounds mirror the wounds of the Crucified.

Soon we joined our hands and prayed the Our Father together (they all seemed to know it). They all took Communion on the tongue. They sipped from the Cup. That table. That meal. It felt like home.

By the final blessing, young men wept and mascara ran down the cheeks of young women. They left the church that morning with great reluctance, holding and hugging each other, seeming thankful there was a place in the world that could make them feel welcome.

SUCH DIZZY NATURAL HAPPINESS

An hour after the memorial Mass for Eric Hamilton had ended, his friends were still in the front of the church, talking, laughing a little, still smoking cigarettes. They didn't want to leave. Clearly, something graceful and powerful was at work. A scattering of teenagers, most of them baptized into the Christian faith but none of whom, I suspected, would say that they had kept many of the rules very well. It didn't matter. Not really. The centrifugal force of their anger or indifference or hostility at the unforgiving world had not flung them too far from their home, their true center. To borrow from Seamus Heaney in his poem *The Cure at Troy*, their outcry, at the time of their choosing, would become a birth-cry. Heaney also wrote this, in the same poem:

History says, don't hope
On this side of the grave.
But then, once in a lifetime
The longed-for tidal wave
Of justice can rise up
And hope and history rhyme.

QUESTIONS FOR REFLECTION AND DISCUSSION

1. Make a list of ten people you love who have died. Do you feel that some or all of them are still alive to you in a real way? Describe what that means to you.

2. What does it mean for us to ask the Father to "deliver us from evil"? What is our role in that delivery, for ourselves and for others?

3. "Eternal life" is not exactly the same as "everlasting life." "Eternal" life has no beginning and no end. It is the life of God, and so there can be no evil there. So what did it mean when the "rich young man" asked Jesus, "Good Master, what must I do to enter into eternal life?" Jesus' answer was: "For you, you must sell everything you have, give the money to the poor, and come follow me." What is the thing that is blocking you from entering into eternal life, right now, today? Reflect and discuss.

CONCLUSION

AMEN

...patch
a few words together and don't try
to make them elaborate, this isn't
a contest but the doorway
into thanks, and a silence in which
another voice may speak.

Mary Oliver, *Prayer*

A few years ago, I was in western Pennsylvania giving a retreat to a convent of religious sisters. Mother Superior came to me one morning and asked if I could hear the confession of one of the sisters who was in their infirmary and then celebrate the anointing of the sick with her. "She's ninety-five years old, Father," she said. "She may have a few days still before God takes her."

I agreed, of course, and later that afternoon I arrived at her door and knocked. I heard no response so I opened the door quietly and walked in. She was resting peacefully in her bed.

She wore a modest white cotton night gown. The sheets were white and starched. The soft blanket, white. Her hair was wispy and white; her face, her folded hands, a blush pink. "Sister," I said, softly. Her eyes opened and she looked up at me. A faint smile appeared. I told her that I heard she wanted to go to Confession and receive the Anointing of the Sick. She nodded.

So I sat down, put on my purple stole and made the sign of the cross. "Bless me, Father," she said, in a voice as light as gossamer, "for I have sinned. This is my last confession."

My God, I thought, *words I have never heard uttered before.* Instantly I felt drawn—no, tugged—toward her by God the Father who, in an instant, had become like one of the nuns I had in grade school who would occasionally catch me drifting off. *Pay attention, Patrick!* God was telling me. I inched toward her. I was leaning into sacred space.

For her penance, I asked her to pray The Our Father. Later I anointed her forehead and hands. "May the Lord, who frees you from sin," I said at the end, "save you and raise you up." One last blessing, a goodbye, and I was off. As I was shutting the door behind me, I heard the sister pray. "Our Father," she said, "who art in Heaven."

The Our Father reminds us with every recitation that we all are making our way to the Father. It is *the* prayer for the journey, taught to us by his Son.

We can plot our path by measuring the distance we have traveled from regret to gratitude, from despair to hope. And when we find ourselves occasionally at the place where hope and gratitude intersect, well, then we can say, "Amen." "Let it be so." "I believe."

The Lord's Prayer will have done its job. And we can rest for a spell in healing, holy, happy silence and listen to what our prodigal Father has in store for us.

APPENDIX

SOME COOL TRANSLATIONS

Untangle the knots within so that we can mend our hearts' simple ties to each other. Don't let surface things delude us.

Neil Douglas-Klotz, *Prayer of the Cosmos*

A PRIMARY SCHOOL'S VERSION
OF THE LORD'S PRAYER

Our Father in heaven, you are awesome!

Show us who you are and how you want us to be.

Make earth more like heaven.

Please give us what we need to keep going each day.

Help us when we are wrong and clean us up
    on the inside.

Help us to let other people off and move on.

Keep us from bad stuff.

You're in charge!

You're strong and powerful and always there.

Forever!

Amen.

From: https://cofewinchester.contentfiles.net/media/assets/
file/Versions_of_The_Lords_Prayer.pdf

THE LORD'S PRAYER, FROM THE ORIGINAL ARAMAIC TRANSLATION

by Neil Douglas-Klotz in *Prayers of the Cosmos*

O Birther! Father-Mother of the Cosmos
Focus your light within us—make it useful.
Create your reign of unity now
Through our fiery hearts and willing hands
Help us love beyond our ideals
and sprout acts of compassion for all creatures.
Animate the earth within us: we then
feel the Wisdom underneath supporting all.
Untangle the knots within
so that we can mend our hearts' simple ties
    to each other.
Don't let surface things delude us,
But free us from what holds us back
    from our true purpose.
Out of you, the astonishing fire,
Returning light and sound to the cosmos.
Amen.

From: https://cofewinchester.contentfiles.net/media/assets/
file/Versions_of_The_Lords_Prayer.pdf

NAZARENE TRANSLITERATION
OF THE LORD'S PRAYER

Oh Thou, from whom the breath of life comes,

who fills all realms of sound, light, and vibration.

May Your light be experienced in my utmost holiest.

Your Heavenly Domain approaches.

Let Your will come true—in the universe

just as on earth.

Give us wisdom for our daily need,

detach the fetters of faults that bind us,

like we let go the guilt of others.

Let us not be lost in superficial things,

but let us be freed from that what keeps us

from our true purpose.

From You comes the all-working will,

the lively strength to act,

the song that beautifies all

and renews itself from age to age.

Sealed in trust, faith, and truth, I confirm

with my entire being.

From: https://cofewinchester.contentfiles.net/media/assets/
file/Versions_of_The_Lords_Prayer.pdf

THE INDIGENOUS LORD'S PRAYER

O Great Father, the One who lives above us all,
Your name is sacred and holy.
Bring your good road to us
For the beauty of the world above is reflected
    in the earth below.
Provide for us day by day the elk, the buffalo, the
    salmon, the corn, the squash, the wild rice,
all those good things we need every day
    to feed our families.
Release us from the things we have done wrong
in the same way we release others for the things
    done wrong to us.
Guide us away from selfish desires that tempt us
    to stray from your good road,
And rescue us from that evil one
    and his worthless ways.

From: rhfoerger.wordpress.com

SUCH DIZZY NATURAL HAPPINESS

HAWAIIAN PIDGIN VERSION

God, you our Fadda. You stay inside da sky.
We like all da peopo know fo shua how you stay,
an dat you stay good an spesho,
an we like dem give you plenny respeck.
We like you come King fo everybody now.
We like everybody make jalike you like,
ova hea inside da world,
jalike da angel guys up inside da sky make
     jalike you like.
Give us da food we need fo today an every day.
Hemo our shame,
an let us go fo all da kine bad stuff we do to you,
jalike us guys let da odda guys go awready,
an we no stay huhu wit dem fo all da kine bad stuff
     dey do to us.
No let us get chance fo do bad kine stuff,
but take us outa dea, so da Bad Guy no can hurt us.
[Cuz you our King, You get da real power,
An you stay awesome foeva.]
Dass it!

From: ministrants.com/lords-prayer.php

MAORI (SOUTH PACIFIC INDIGENOUS) VERSION

Earth-maker, life-giver, pain-bearer,
Source of all that is and all that shall be,
Father and Mother of us all,
Loving God in whom is heaven:

May the hallowing of your name
echo through the universe!
May your heavenly will be done
by all creatures great and small!
And may your commonwealth
of peace and freedom
sustain our hope and come on earth!

With the bread we need this day, feed us.
For the hurt we inflict on one another, forgive us.
By your grace and mercy,
strengthen us through times of temptation,
and spare us from trials too great to endure.
Free us from bigotry and evil, for service and truth.
For you reign in the glory of the power that is Love.
    Amen.

From: https://www.ccdurham.org/two-versions-of-lords-prayer/

THE LORD'S PRAYER IN AMERICAN SIGN LANGUAGE (ASL)

From: https://www.youtube.com/watch?v=xEitKUXi3Pw

BOOKS ON SPIRITUAL TRANSFORMATION

The Geography of God's Mercy
and
The Long Yearning's End
by Patrick Hannon, CSC

Awaken the Stars: What We REALLY Teach
edited by Shannon Mayer and Jacquie Van Hoomissen

Cat's Foot, A Novel
by Brian Doyle

Confessions of an Ugly-Bible Reader
The Grace of Praying with the Scriptures Daily,
Coffee Stains and All
by Tim McCormick

Full Circle
A Quest for Transformation
by Juan-Lorenzo Hinojosa and Raven Hinojosa

Stories
by John Shea

Near Occasions of Hope
A Woman's Glimpse of a Church That Can Be
by Karen E. Eifler

Available from booksellers or
www.actapublications.com, 800-397-2282

POETRY AND PRAYER

Leaps of Faith
Playful Poems and Fanciful Photos
by Sister Marva Hoeckelman, OSB

The Merton Prayer
An Exercise in Authenticity
by Steven A. Denny

Prayers from Around the World and Across the Ages
by Victor M. Parachin

The Return of Sunshine
Poems by a Laureate for Ecstatic Grandparents
by Norbert Krapf

The Soul of Teaching
Encouragement for High School Teachers and Principals,
Who Sometimes Might Need It
by John Horan, drawings by Mary Horan

We Knew No Mortality
Memories of Our Spiritual Home,
Poetry and Prose
by Robert Eric Shoemaker, photos Sara Shoemaker

Where God Is at Home
Poems of God's Word and World
by Irene Zimmerman, OSF, photos James Behrens, OCSO

Available from booksellers or
www.actapublications.com, 800-397-2282

FINDING DIVINE PRESENCE
IN DAILY LIFE

Interrupted Presence
Stories of Finding Faith in Times of Trouble
by Clarissa Valbuena Aljentera, Stuart Wilson-Smith,
Danielle R. Ayodele, Mariam Pera, Marlon Bobier Vargas,
Natalie Crary, Darius A. Villalobos, Marissa Butler, Isaac
Garcia, Vivian Cabrera, Mark Evans Piper

Unexpected Presence
Stories of Surprising Encounters
by Charlotte Bruny, Alice Camille, Patrick Cassidy, Dave
Fortier, Fred Hang, Patrick Hannon, Kathleen McGrory,
Don Paglia, Kathleen Parulski, Greg Pierce, Bill Spielberger,
Katie Walsh

Diamond Presence
Stories of Finding God at the Old Ball Park
by Carol DeChant, Andre Dubus, William John Fitzgerald,
Patrick Hannon, Sara Kaden, Jean Larkin, Jerome Lamb,
Helen Lambin, Michael Leach, Robert Raccuglia, Patrick
Reardon, Michael Wilt

Hidden Presence
Stories of Blessings That Transformed Sorrow or Loss
by James Behrens, Alice Camille, Kass Dotterweich, Patrick
Hannon, Helen Lambin, Michael Leach, Terry Nelson-
Johnson, Robert Raccuglia, Patrick Reardon, Joyce Rupp,
Joni Woelfel, Vinita Wright

Christmas Presence
Gifts That Were More Than They Seemed
by James Behrens, Alice Camille, Carol DeChant, Kass
Dotterweich, Fred Hang, Patrick Hannon, Michael Leach,
Tom McGrath, Patrick Reardon, John Shea, Joni Woelfel,
Vinita Wright

Available from booksellers or
www.actapublications.com, 800-397-2282

LITERARY PORTALS TO PRAYER

(Illuminated by *The Message* Bible)

Louisa May Alcott by Susan Bailey

Hans Christian Andersen by Mary K. Doyle

Jane Austen by Rachel Hart Winter

Elizabeth Barrett Browning by Joyce Brinkman

Charles Dickens by Jon M. Sweeney

George Eliot by Darren J.N. Middleton

Elizabeth Gaskell by Patricia Lynch

Herman Melville by Paul Boudreau

William Shakespeare by Ron Marasco

Edith Wharton by Patrick T. Reardon

Walt Whitman by Norbert Krapf

Available from booksellers or
www.actapublications.com, 800-397-2282

ADVANCE PRAISE FOR
SUCH DIZZY NATURAL HAPPINESS

You may come for the stories and linger with the witty observations and cornucopia of quotables. But don't be surprised if you learn something too, something you already knew but didn't know you knew until Fr. Pat dredged it up from your depths.

—Alice Camille, scripture columnist for *U.S. Catholic* magazine,
  and co-author, *The Forgiveness Book*

Profound yet practical insights about God's personal care for every aspect of our imperfect lives. In a world where online followers can "love" us one minute and "cancel" us the next, *Such Dizzy Natural Happiness* is a refreshing reminder that The Lord's Prayer reveals our *true* value and worth that, hopefully and graciously we extend to others.

—Kimberly Fletcher, editor/publisher, evangelical Christian books

Too many tepid repetitions of words—and too many cherished traditions abruptly cancelled—can singe a soul. The young people I work with need the joy, wonder, pathos, and hope that pervade *Such Dizzy Natural Happiness;* it will rouse them from taking precious things for granted.

—Karen Eifler, professor of English and author, *Near Occasions of Hope: A Woman's Glimpse of a Church That Can Be*

What do I think of *Such Dizzy Natural Happiness*? First off, it's difficult *not* to think about it. Secondly, I've made notes to reflect upon, to not forget, to go back to, to tie together, to reread, to question, to see where I qualify, and to wander through and wonder about. It's testing my religiosity versus my spirituality.

—Lawrence McCarthy, retired teacher and author, *Chalk-Talk: Vignettes from Three Decades of Teaching in the Inner City*